THE OFFICIAL
SHERLOCK
PUZZLE BOOK

THE OFFICIAL
SHERLOCK
PUZZLE BOOK

CHRIS MASLANKA
AND STEVE TRIBE

CHRONICLE BOOKS
San Francisco

First published in Great Britain in 2017 by BBC Books

First published in the United States of America in 2018 by Chronicle Books LLC

Text copyright © 2018 by Chris Maslanka and Steve Tribe
Design copyright © 2018 by Woodland Books

Library of Congress Cataloging-in-Publication Data available.
ISBN 978-1-4521-7314-6

Manufactured in China.

Cover design by Woodland Books

Chronicle Books LLC
680 Second Street
San Francisco, CA 94107
www.chroniclebooks.com

10 9 8 7 6 5 4 3 2

CONTENTS

Introduction | VI

A Study in Pink | 1
Solutions | 15

The Blind Banker | 27
Solutions | 42

The Great Game | 53
Solutions | 64

A Scandal in Belgravia | 77
Solutions | 90

The Hounds of Baskerville | 97
Solutions | 107

The Reichenbach Fall | 115
Solutions | 124

Many Happy Returns | 131
Solutions | 141

The Empty Hearse | 149
Solutions | 156

The Sign of Three | 161
Solutions | 169

His Last Vow | 177
Solutions | 182

The Abominable Bride | 187
Solutions | 203

The Six Thatchers | 213
Solutions | 221

The Lying Detective | 227
Solutions | 238

The Final Problem | 245
Solutions | 253

Acknowledgements | 261

Introduction

'There is no puzzle, no enigma, that my friend Sherlock cannot solve.'

You are about to encounter about 200 questions and challenges, based on or inspired by the BBC series *Sherlock*. There are rebus and picture puzzles to test your observational skills, and matchstick puzzles that ask you to rearrange what you have closely observed. There are word games – cryptic crossword clues, anagrams and acrostics – in which the answer is always right in front of you, if you know how to look. Codebreaking and cryptograms will exercise your ability to detect patterns in words, letters, symbols and numbers, while mathematical puzzles will stretch your arithmetical skills. Then there are the brain teasers and the logic problems, sometimes impenetrable riddles requiring you to exert all your deductive muscles. Lateral thinking is key, and comes into play in a great many puzzles here, just as it does in the series itself.

We've included some quiz questions, too, checking your recall of the detail of the television episodes. And also, possibly, giving your brain some respite. Every so often, you'll come across a puzzle that seems simple and straightforward – probably because it is (relatively). Why? Well, first, so nobody leaves empty-handed. Second, because sometimes a puzzle is purely asking you to appreciate a point. And third, of course, so you too can share Sherlock's peculiar combination of smug glee and bewildered amazement that something so self-evident (to him, and you) could be so baffling to everybody else.

'I've sent you a little puzzle... just to say hi.'

Unless you truly can think like Sherlock, chances are you'll look at a lot of these conundrums for the first time and find yourself giving them a firmly blank stare. But there'll also be plenty of occasions when you're delighted to have immediately spotted precisely the correct reasoning to solve a particular problem. Not only that, you're happily confident you've got the arithmetic right. Delight and confidence can be an irresistibly heady mix, and you promptly announce your answer to yourself, or even to some unsuspecting bystander or appreciative amanuensis.

Later, you check the real answer, and you're dismayed to realize that you're some way out. Quite some way out. Your calculations are spot on, as far as they go, and you really have alighted on precisely the correct reasoning, but you've completely failed to follow that reasoning through to its logical conclusion.

Always follow the reasoning all the way to the end. And then check back to make sure that you have – before you leap onto the Baker Street sofa yelling, 'Spot on... I didn't expect to be right about everything!'

And now we'll give you a puzzle and watch you dance.

A STUDY
IN PINK

1
Rebus

The adventure began with this (9)

2
Upside Downside

As he left his therapist, John reflected that his ability to read upside down had its uses. He had been able to read what she had written on her pad: 'Still has trust issues.'

Mind you, the same skill had almost got him killed crossing the road, after he swapped the sands of Afghanistan for the busy streets of London. How might that have happened?

3
The Two Beakers

'Quick – get me exactly 40 cc of water from that tap,' barked Sherlock, gesturing towards Molly without taking his eyes from the microscope. 'Hurry.'

Molly rushed over to the sink. 'Exactly 40 cc?'

'Yes, yes, 40 cc, precisely, now!'

'Beakers...' muttered Molly. 'Unmarked, fantastic.' She picked up a 30 cc beaker, and a larger 50 cc beaker. 'A bit of judicious juggling...'

'Water!'

Molly started filling one beaker from the tap, then pouring some of the water into the other beaker and some into the sink and so on, in various combinations. Then she carried exactly 40 cc of water to Sherlock, who promptly drank it.

'Not bad,' conceded Sherlock. 'But you did it in eight moves, and you could have done it in six. Come to think of it, you could have done it a lot more simply.'

How had Molly done it?

How could it have been done in six moves?

How could it be done with even less fuss?

4
The Cabbie

John took what few personal effects he had to 221B Baker Street by cab. He rummaged for the fare, which happened to be a whole number of pounds, which should have been fine as he had a whole number of pounds in each pocket. But the amount in his left-hand trouser pocket was £22 too little; the amount in his right-hand trouser pocket was £2 too little; in fact even the total sum was too little to pay the fare. What *was* the fare?

5
Quiz

(a) Speaking of personal effects, what does *In Arduis Fidelis* mean on Watson's mug?

(b) Watson's limp – which leg?

(c) How does Sherlock like his coffee?

(d) How many people had the cabbie killed before he got around to Sherlock?

6
The Game Is On

Sherlock bounded down the last flight of stairs into the hallway of 221B Baker Street four steps at a time; there were three steps left over. John came down three at a time; there were two left over.

What is the minimum number of steps there could be?

What is the second smallest number of steps that would give the same remainders?

7
A Stepwise Transition

John could almost see the cogs in Sherlock's brain go cranking around a click at a time as he assimilated the idea that John's sibling was not a sister but a brother.

Change BROTHER to SISTER in as few moves as possible, with each move changing a letter, adding one or taking one away, and at every stage making a valid word.

8
Stepping Out

Sherlock and John raced out of Angelo's in pursuit of a suspect cab. As they turned into one street they were both on their left foot, but John was managing only four steps to Sherlock's five. When – if they kept up this pace like clockwork – would their right feet both strike the ground at the same time?

9
Catching a Taxi

In an adrenalin-fuelled chase through the diversions, roadworks, jams and one-way systems that London affords the motorist, Sherlock and John dive down narrow streets, scale ladders and fire escapes, and jump roofs to try to head off a receding taxi.

As they descend a conventional spiral staircase, viewed from street level, are they going clockwise or anticlockwise?

IO
A Three-Patch Problem

Here are three nicotine patches. How many times the perimeter of one patch is the (outer) perimeter of all three?

II
Patchwork

'There are two-patch cases,' remarked Sherlock, 'and there are three-patch cases. This is a three-patch case. Might even be a four.'

In the following sum, each of the letters stands for a digit from 1 to 9 inclusive and different letters stand for different digits throughout.

$$
\begin{array}{r}
\text{PATCH} \\
+ \text{PATCH} \\
\hline
\text{CASES}
\end{array}
$$

What number is represented by PATCHES?

12
Enigma

Lestrade has a nicotine patch on his arm. Why does it not increase his crime-solving abilities?

13
Cryptic Clues

(a) It gratifies the loaf-maker, we hear, where Mrs Hudson lives (5, 6)

(b) PA having three articles to her name (6)

(c) Sherlockian method of racing taxis through recreational area – a breathless hour (7)

(d) An answer you might find in Molly's lab? (8)

(e) Another answer you might find in Molly's lab? (6)

(f) Crime scoop obtained by means of forensic device? (10)

(g) Delete every second letter from this device of Sherlock's to get baker (10)

(h) Confused narrow atheist in John's family (7, 6)

14
Taking the Biscuit

'I'm your landlady, dear, not your housekeeper.'

'Have a heart, Mrs Hudson – I'm in shock.' Sherlock grabbed a blanket from the armchair and pulled it tightly round his shoulders. 'Just a cup of tea.'

'I'll give you a shock, young man.' Mrs Hudson vanished back into the kitchen and put the kettle on.

'And maybe some biscuits,' Sherlock called.

'I still don't see how you could be sure the case would be pink,' mused John.

'Listen, John. I didn't *know* the case would be pink; it just seemed a good bet, given that practically everything else about her was pink. You need to act on probabilities and patterns. But patterns can be misleading, so you do have to keep revising your views as you go along. Keep it fluid. To give you an admittedly rather contrived example, if I give you this sequence of symbols...'

Sherlock paused to tap a sequence into his iPad:

111111111111111111111★111

'I've replaced one symbol with a star. What's the missing symbol?'

'Well, "1", obviously. I don't see what else there is to go on.'

Sherlock laughed. 'Yes, but that's dull! The only way the question becomes interesting is if the missing symbol is *not* "1". So in that case – what is it?'

John gazed levelly at Sherlock.

'Think John, think!' insisted Sherlock. 'There are twenty-six of them! Twenty-six! What do they represent?'

'A flock of large white birds recently taken ill in Regent's Park?'

'Very droll,' said Sherlock.

Come up with a rationale for why it's not 1.

I5
A Bitter Pill

When Lestrade's team searched the home of the late Jeff Hope, they discovered three little bottles, each containing two pills.

The label on the first bottle read 'Both Poisonous'. The label on the second bottle read 'Both Harmless'. The label on the third bottle read 'One Poisonous, One Harmless'.

Sherlock theorised – correctly – that Hope had muddled up the labels so that each bottle carried the wrong label. The question then was, which bottle should you plump for to maximise your chances of *not* picking a poison pill?

I6
Oddly Enough

'But Jeff Hope knew that most people don't think,' reasoned Sherlock. 'I can calculate odds, but you, Lestrade...'

John sighed. 'Sorry, Greg. He's about to show us how stupid we are,' he said, offering Sherlock a 50p piece.

'Good, John. You see? You're starting to think. Now! If I flip this coin ten times which is a more likely result?*

HHHHHHHHHH

or:

HTTTHTHTTH?'

('H' stands for 'head', 'T' for 'tails'.)

Paradise Lost

'They say that Eden was perfect until the devil got in.' It had taken Sherlock a single glance at Mrs Hudson's wordsearch (Win A Holiday for Two!) in the *Evening Standard*. What had leapt out at him?

B	E	G	U	N	I	C	H	O	L	T	K	C
E	S	C	H	S	C	H	O	L	T	Z	I	A
G	E	R	A	N	I	U	M	I	J	A	N	R
O	V	O	R	T	A	R	A	J	O	L	G	N
N	O	V	E	N	M	S	G	A	P	I	C	A
I	R	I	B	U	S	O	M	S	I	C	U	T
A	S	T	E	R	O	G	R	M	N	Y	P	I
B	D	T	L	I	T	L	E	I	O	N	A	O
B	A	L	L	A	D	O	N	N	A	A	L	N
A	F	O	X	G	L	O	V	E	I	R	I	T
E	S	T	A	Q	I	D	O	X	R	G	T	O
S	T	I	P	P	L	L	S	N	I	O	O	Y
S	D	A	I	S	Y	E	O	A	S	L	S	E

Second Sitting

Back at Angelo's, John and Sherlock tucked into the free meal that had been interrupted.

'Is it true what you said about Angelo?'

'Yes. Lestrade was clutching at straws, needed an arrest. If the police had had their way, Angelo would be rotting in a cell right now.'

'Instead of cooking this amazing lasagne.'

'Precisely. Rehabilitation, with a side order of garlic bread.' Sherlock laid out thirteen toothpicks on the table to make four cells. 'I'll give you until the coffee arrives to make the former profession of our host. And if you manage that, you can follow it up by moving just two of the toothpicks to make his current profession.'

What were the two professions Sherlock was alluding to?

19
Rebus

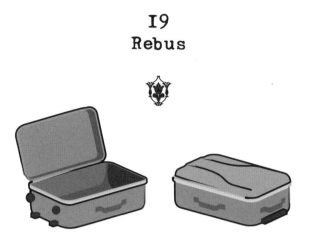

What *A Study in Pink* was not! (2, 4, 3, 4, 4)

20
Not a Fan, Then

A ping announced a message on Sherlock's phone. 'It seems not everyone is a fan,' he laughed, and showed it to John.

> ZPV DBMM ZPVSTFMG B DPOTVMUJOH EFUFDUJWF
> CVU J DBMM ZPV BO JOTVMUJOH EFGGFDUJWF

'What does it mean?'

'It's a simple substitution cipher; *really* simple, actually. You see the similarity between the words in the first part and the words in the second?'

What does the message mean?

SOLUTIONS

I
Rebus

Flat share (flats + hare)

2
Upside Downside

When crossing Bickenhall Street (a one-way street), he read the writing on the tarmac on the opposite side of the road: 'Look Left'. He automatically did so, started to cross, and was nearly knocked down by a car coming from the right.

3
Two Beakers

Molly did the following:

1. Fill the small beaker; it now contains 30 cc.

2. Transfer the contents of the small beaker to the large one; the large one now contains 30 cc.

3. Fill the small beaker again; now both beakers contain 30 cc.

4. Fill the large beaker from the small; there are now 10 cc in the small beaker and 50 cc in the large.

5. Pour the contents of the large beaker away.

6. Transfer the 10cc from the small beaker to the large; now the small beaker is empty and the large one contains 10 cc.

7. Fill the small beaker again; now the small beaker contains 30 cc and the large one contains 10 cc.

8. Transfer the 30 cc from the small beaker to the large beaker; it now contains 40 cc.

Sherlock was right that it could be done in fewer moves, but then he wasn't the one being flustered by his imperious commands.

1. Fill the larger beaker; it now contains 50 cc.

2. Fill the smaller one from the larger; there are now 30 cc in the small one and 20 cc left in the large one.

3. Empty the smaller beaker.

4. Pour the 20 cc left in the large beaker into the small one.

5. Fill the larger beaker; it now contains 50 cc, and the smaller still has 20 cc in it.

6. Top up the smaller beaker from the larger; there are now 30 cc in the small beaker and 40 cc in the large one.

Sherlock was also right that this is the smallest number of moves you can do it in if you use this technique, involving just six moves (with the option of a seventh if you believe in tidying up after yourself, which Sherlock really doesn't).

But then he thought of the following, far neater procedure which cuts out all the shuffling: fill the smaller beaker and tilt it slowly. Water will spill out, of course, but ignore that for the present. The surface starts as a circle and becomes a more and more elongated ellipse as you tilt it. When one end of this ellipse touches a point where the side of the beaker meets the bottom, and the other end of the ellipse just touches the rim of the beaker, the beaker is exactly half full of water (by symmetry!). That is, it contains 15 cc. Now do the same for the other and you have 25 cc. Pour the 15 cc into the larger beaker and voila – you have 15 + 25 cc = 40 cc, as required.

4

The Cabbie

£23. If the fare is f in pounds, then in one pocket he has $f - 22$; and in the other $f - 2$. As he has something in both pockets, we know that the fare is greater than 22. But we also know that $(f - 22) + (f - 2) < f$, as the total is too little to pay the fare. That is $2f - 24 < f$, which boils down to: $f < 24$. There's only one whole number less than 24 and more than 22: and that's 23.

5

Quiz

(a) 'Faithful in Adversity'. It's the motto of the Royal Army Medical Corps.

(b) Right leg.

(c) He tells Molly he wants it black with two sugars.

(d) From Hope's words: 'I didn't kill those four people, Mr Holmes.' And he has no reason to lie. Of course if it were purely random, his surviving until his meeting with Sherlock would have had only a 6.25 per cent chance.

6
The Game Is On

Eleven steps.

Imagine there were no steps left over; then the smallest number would be twelve steps. If you reduce that number by 1, you get a remainder of 3 when the number of steps is divided by 4, and a remainder of 2 when it is divided by 3.

The second smallest number of stairs would be 23: if you add on any multiple of 12 to 11 you will get the same remainders.

7
A Stepwise Transition

BROTHER – BOTHER – BATHER – BATTER – BITTER – SITTER – SISTER.

Can you do better?

8
Stepping Out

Never. For each group of five of Sherlock's steps, only the first occurs at the same time as one of John's group of four steps – the first.

In the first such cycle (a cycle being four steps of John's and five steps of Sherlock's), Sherlock's first step is a left, and John's first step is also a left. In the second cycle, Sherlock's first step is a right (because he has made an odd number of steps in the first cycle), but John's is a left (as he has made an even number of steps in the first cycle). Then, with the next cycle, we are in the same relative position as we were in at the outset...

So, although their left steps exactly coincide periodically, and Sherlock's right step coincides periodically with John's left step, they never put their right feet down at exactly the same time.

A musical analogy might be of help. Imagine each footfall is a musical beat:

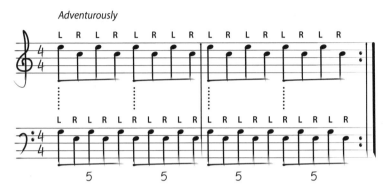

John's steps are shown in the upper line, Sherlock's on the bottom. Note that Sherlock 'plays five notes' in the same time as John 'plays four notes'.

Point to Ponder: Does Sherlock's left foot ever hit the pavement at the same time as John's right foot?

9
Catching a Taxi

Clockwise.

A standard spiral staircase follows the convention established in the construction of a medieval castle keep. The intention was to disadvantage the (generally) right-handed swordsman trying to gain access from below, while the owner (the builder) defended the keep from above. As a result, you went down anticlockwise as seen from above, leading with your sword in your right hand. The attacker trying to ascend from below was forced to use his left hand or have his right hand cramped against the axis of the stairwell, restricting his blows.

So, seen from above, you would be going anticlockwise as you descended, and clockwise as seen from below.

10
A Three-Patch Problem

Two and a half.

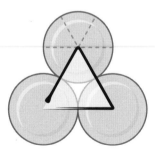

Draw a triangle with its corners at the centre of each circle. As the triangle is equilateral, each angle will be 60°, so the fraction of each patch's circumference that falls within the triangle is ⅙ (60 ÷ 360 = ⅙).

Therefore we need to subtract 3 x ⅙ from the total perimeter of all 3 patches to find the total outer perimeter.

II
Patchwork

The sum is:

$$
\begin{array}{r}
19732 \\
+\,19732 \\
\hline
39464
\end{array}
$$

PATCHES = 1973264.

I2
Enigma

Because it's not a patch on Sherlock.

I3
Cryptic Clues

(a) Baker Street (baker's treat)

(b) Anthea (An + the + a)

(c) Parkour (park + 'our)

(d) Solution

(e) Retort (a glass container with a long neck, used in distilling liquids and other chemical operations)

(f) Microscope

(g) BLACKBERRY

(h) Harriet Watson

14
Taking the Biscuit

'That, John,' said Sherlock as he gulped down the last of his tea, 'is the list of the number of syllables in the names of the letters of the alphabet – in order.'

John's dubious expression shifted towards irritation.

'Well, I didn't say it would be an edifying answer,' Sherlock told him. 'I just said one can be lulled into a false sense of security by patterns. There can always be an unexpected "double-u".'

15
A Bitter Pill

If you choose the bottle labelled 'Both Poisonous', you have a 3/4 (75 per cent) chance of a happy outcome.

If PP stands for 'Both Poisonous', 'HP' stands for 'One Poisonous, One Harmless' and 'HH' stands for 'Both Harmless', these are the only possible situations:

PP	HH	HP
HH	PH	PP
PH	PP	HH

(The top line refers to the labels; the bottom two lines the contents.)

16

Oddly Enough

The probabilities of a head or tail are equal; so the chances (before you start) of getting either run when you flip the coin ten times are exactly the same.

Point to Ponder: What are those chances?

17

Paradise Lost

Among all those flowers, there was just one snake in the grass – by the name of Moriarty.

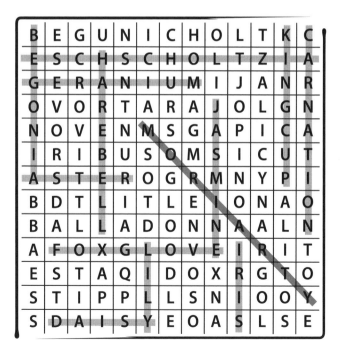

18
Second Sitting

He was a THIEF and became a CHEF.

19
Rebus

An open and shut case.

20
Not a Fan, Then

If you shift each letter one earlier in the alphabet, you get:

YOU CALL YOURSELF A CONSULTING DETECTIVE
BUT I CALL YOU AN INSULTING DEFECTIVE.

THE
BLIND
BANKER

I
Gifted Germans

John slept well and woke refreshed. He looked contentedly around the flat, and thought to himself that, despite Sherlock's antics, he might well have found his place at last.

Mind you, this was before he found the festering paw that was part of Sherlock's current experiment. *That* shock was to come. When he entered the kitchen, he just saw that the few remaining fridge magnets on the fridge door had now been rearranged. Yesterday, they'd read:

'MON – SAT.'

What did it now say?

2
The Shirt Off His Back

'It's not going to work, Mrs Hudson!' exploded Sherlock.

'Oh, Sherlock – at least let me try!' wailed Mrs Hudson.

'Excuse me.' John was standing in the doorway. 'What's going on?'

'John, dear, thank heavens. You talk to him. Try and make him see reason.'

'Reason? Ha! For reasons best known to herself, Mrs Hudson has decided to ensure I have a fresh shirt every day.'

'Outrageous,' said John. 'I can see why you'd be upset.'

'I've got a plan and everything,' Mrs Hudson told him. 'Every Friday morning, I'll take a week's worth of shirts to the launderette and pick up the load I left the previous Friday.'

'It's a stupid plan,' shouted Sherlock. 'It will fall at the first fence.'

'Especially as he's only got five shirts,' said John.

What is the minimum number of shirts Sherlock needs for Mrs Hudson's plan to succeed?

3
Astronomy

'What's *that*?' demanded Sherlock, pointing at where his favourite bit of wallpaper had been.

'It's called a constellation,' retorted John. 'Of stars. The Great Bear. I've decided it's my turn to educate you, since you don't seem to know what makes the world go round. Or even *that* the world goes round.'

'Seriously, John?' snapped Sherlock. 'That *again*? I've told you: it's not important. I only keep what's important. All that matters is the work. What possible use could any of that be to someone like me? As if there could be someone like me. Stars are up there out of the way for a reason. And besides, stars from the same constellation aren't even near each other – they're all at quite different distances from us. It's illogical that people speak of them as being in the same constellation at all.'

Sherlock grabbed a pen, jumped onto the couch and drew three straight lines on the picture of the Great Bear. The three lines divided each star in the constellation from every other one.

Using just three straight lines, separate each star of the Great Bear from each and every other star in it.

4
A Little Light Housework
— from John's Blog

Sherlock is not one for domestic routine, so I was quite shocked the day he appeared at my side by the kitchen sink, brandishing a tea towel and drying the dishes. With Sherlock Holmes, some things you just don't comment on, so I went on with the washing-up, eyes front, not a word.

Then I realised that he was off in his own little world again, not so much as glancing at the plates he was wiping. He was putting them away without setting eye on them. Which at least meant I now understood what he was up to drying dishes – he was showing off.

Eyes front.

Once he'd given up and slouched off, I looked in the cupboard. The plates were of two very similar sizes – I could only tell the difference by comparing their lengths edgeways. As he'd dried, Sherlock had stacked each plate on the shelf, without examining it, somehow managing to sort all the plates into the two kinds, with the slightly smaller plates on top and the slightly larger ones underneath. How was that possible?

5
Clues to Solve?

'Oh, Sherlock, you won't be happy until there's a triple murder, will you?' said Mrs Hudson sympathetically. 'It's like the puzzle in the *Evening Standard* yesterday: "Take CLUES to SOLVE in as few moves as possible with each move changing one letter and with each move making a valid word."'

6
Cryptic Clues

John looked concerned. 'Everything OK, Mrs Hudson?'

'Not really, dear, no.'

'Can I help? I *am* a doctor...'

'Oh, it's just they've changed it, and I can't finish it any more. I used to like to do the crossword in the afternoon with a nice cuppa, but now it's like something from one of your blogs. I mean, just take a look at these clues...'

(a) Loner may be regenerated in this part of London? (10)

(b) Catch sight of friend returning with essential digital devices? (7)

(c) To Ghent to form a secret society (3, 4)

(d) Pith resides in these in Molly's lab? (5, 6)

7
Grand Theft Automated

While John was fighting the automated checkout at the supermarket, Sherlock was fighting a Sikh warrior. Sherlock emerged unscathed, apart from a scratch on the table. He made a mental note to send John to the supermarket to get some of that stuff for covering up scratches before Mrs Hudson saw it. All that fuss – all over the Jaria diamond.

The Jaria diamond had vanished when the owner went for a drink and showed it off to the assembled company. The police had decided that the thief must have put the diamond in his drink and this had rendered it invisible. Is that possible?

8
Trouble with Nils

At Shad Sanderson investment bank, not all of Sebastian's onetime uni chums were as quick off the mark as Sherlock. As a favour, Seb had given his chum Nils a job in Client Accounts, but he was now regretting his own magnanimity. This morning, instead of relying on the software in the computer, Nils had actually taken out a calculator to add two whole numbers of pounds, and somehow managed to multiply the two numbers instead of adding them. As a result he had ended up with a short billion (a thousand million), when the real total should have been just shy of two million. Rather odd, really, reflected Seb, that two numbers neither of which contained a zero should when multiplied produce a number consisting – apart from the initial 1 – of nothing but zeroes!

What should the correct total have been?

9
Rebus

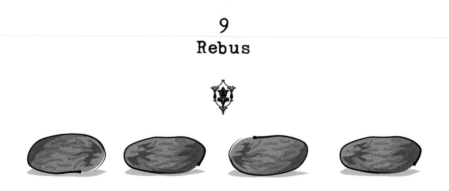

What Sebastian crossed twice, apparently (8)

IO
The Mystery of Sebastian's Watch

'Hang on.' John was typing up his blog. 'You said he crossed the Date Line twice. But if you cross the Date Line twice, it doesn't add two days to your watch. If it did it would mean we could time travel into the future.'

'But we do travel into the future,' answered Sherlock. 'At a rate of one day per day. Dull and inescapable.'

'Ha ha, very clever,' persevered John. 'But am I right, or am I right?'

Well?

II
Rebus

ABCDEFGHIJKLMNOPQRSTUVWXYZ

It contained the key to the cipher (1–1).

12
The East of London

Identify the place given that each asterisk represents a missing letter:

C*I*A*O*

(Although they are unlikely to say CIAO here!)

13
At the Circus

'Are you enjoying it, Sherlock?' asked Sarah. She didn't seem to mind Sherlock being a bit of a gooseberry as much as John did.

'Oh yes,' he replied, as he scanned the crowd. 'I particularly liked the bit where they walk backwards and go forwards.'

What was he on about?

I4
A Playful Number

After this case Sherlock modified his website and included the following symbols in relation to what piece of work?

I5
The Sands of Time

Setting up her act, General Shan carefully prepared four bags of sand. (Well, timing is everything.) Weighing them two at a time (the scales didn't register light weights very accurately), she found the following readings: 3.25, 3.75, 4 (twice), 4.25 and 4.75 – all weights in kilos.

What are the individual weights of the four sandbags?

16
A Bolt from the Blue

After this case was cleared, Detective Inspector Dimmock was (grudgingly) grateful enough to – against his better judgement – accede to Sherlock's request to have a shot with General Shan's crossbow. 'All right, but let me have a go first. And let's skip all that fancy stuff with bags of sand,' he said.

They set up a target and allowed themselves three goes each. Dimmock's first shot hit the edge of the target. The second was closer to the bullseye. 'Now I'm getting the hang of it. Just watch – my third shot will be even better.'

'I think you'll find it's fairly random, Dummock.'

'Dimmock. Hang on, what difference would that make?'

'We need to think of it in proba-*ballistic* terms.'

'That is a terrible pun!' interposed John.

'I have worse.'

'OK. Let's number the bolts 1, 2 and 3. And imagine we list them in order of closeness to the bullseye. Then we have six ways to order the numbers 1, 2 and 3, and in two of them 3 is the first digit, so my chances should be 2/6 or 1/3.' Dimmock pulled the trigger, and the bolt went straight through the window of the waiting squad car.

'Oh dear,' laughed Sherlock. 'Damaging police property!'

Was Dimmock right in his assessment of the probability, though?

17
Intrusive Thoughts

'My problem has never been a shortage of ideas, but the exact opposite: too many thoughts. I have to ignore the distractions and keep out the irrelevancies. A tiny example for you: when I looked down from Van Coon's balcony, I spotted the sign opposite saying "Bar Club Grill", and immediately noticed that if you add a letter to the first word, delete one from the second and add two to the third, you get two animals.'

'Not three?' asked Dimmock.

'No, one of them might even be human if there were three. This was clearly irrelevant to the investigation, so I had to blot it out. Do you have any idea how difficult it is to un-think a thought once you've had it? That's why I am so careful not to stuff my head with unnecessary information. And that, Inspector, is why I would very much appreciate it if you would *shut up.*'

What were the animals?

18
From John's Blog

... He asked the bloke who had been sleeping opposite 221B to keep an eye on the door. 'Give him a pound, John,' he said grandly.

Feeling like an Equerry to the Queen – in fact, I might have said something along those lines to Sherlock – I pulled the change from my pocket and found that, although I had over a pound, none of the coins was a whole number of pounds and it was impossible to make up exactly a pound.

You know what Sherlock's like: for a brief moment, I thought that was important. Then I realised he just meant, 'Give the man some change.' So I gave him all of it.

As I pursued Sherlock, who was by now racing off in the direction of Regent's Park, I found myself wondering what was the maximum sum I might have handed over. Oh god. I've caught some sort of deduction bug...

19
Acrostic

If you write the answers to the clues horizontally in the order given, the first and last letters each spell out the words clued in the Lights.

Clues (across)

1. Ditto (5)

2. The sort of evening John hoped for in *The Blind Banker*? (8)

3. Hard water? (3)

4. What Sherlock thinks Anderson is (5)

5. You need a good one for the lights (3)

Lights (down)

Van Coon's flat, for example (5, 5)

SOLUTIONS

I
Gifted Germans

John found that the magnets had been rearranged to read 'WATSON!'.

'Gifted Germans', by the way, is just an anagram of fridge magnets. Did you spot that?

2
The Shirt Off His Back

Fifteen.

When Mrs Hudson takes some of Sherlock's shirts to the launderette, they will be out of action for just over a week from the time she leaves 221B Baker Street to the time it takes her to collect them and bring them back again. In that time Sherlock will need eight shirts, unless he is to be shirtless while Mrs Hudson goes to fetch the shirts. Of course, he could get around this by swanning around the flat in a dressing gown until she gets back. But what if he had to rush out on a case? He'd be shirt-locked.

A little table makes this clear. We will start the week on a Friday and number the shirts individually, just to keep track of them:

Day (Week 1):	F	S	S	M	T	W	T
Shirt worn:	1	2	3	4	5	6	7

Day (Week 2):	F	S	S	M	T	W	T
Shirt worn:	8*	9	10	11	12	13	14

Day (Week 3):	F	S	S	M	T	W	T
Shirt worn:	15*	1	2	3	4	5	6

8* *On this day, Sherlock dons shirt 8. Later that morning, Mrs Hudson takes shirts 1–7 to the launderette.*

15* *On this day, Sherlock has no choice but to don a fifteenth shirt or be shirtless while Mrs Hudson takes shirts 8–14 inclusive to the launderette and collects clean shirts 1–7 inclusive.*

Note also that because of the necessity of a fifteenth shirt, the number of the shirt you wear gets out of step, which can be distressing to the orderly mind if you pay attention to that sort of thing. You could wear the fifteenth shirt in the morning of Day 15, then switch to the first shirt after lunch but, after a while, two of your fifteen shirts will start to look far less worn than the other thirteen.

Which just goes to show how complicated and tedious even the shirt part of any systematic laundry arrangements can be. This is probably why any creative thinker would prefer to spend that time thinking of things of more consequence.

3
Astronomy

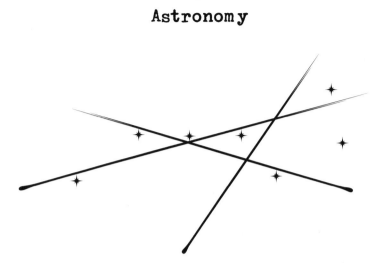

Three straight lines that all cross each other through the same point divide space up into six regions, and we need seven, as there are seven stars in the Great Bear. We need to make sure the lines all cross each other but in such a way they don't all go through the same single point. Sherlock managed this as shown. Actually the stars are arranged in quite a long shape and he was hard put to fit the lines in.

Point to Ponder: Can you always find an arrangement of three straight lines that will separate seven stars no matter how they are arranged?

4
A Little Light Housework

Sherlock didn't look at the plate he was drying at all. He looked at the point in the stack of plates in the cupboard where the slightly larger plates gave way to the slightly smaller ones. This was easy to spot as their being in a stack in the eye-level cupboard meant he was already looking at the stack from the side. He then placed the plate he was drying at this junction between the bigger and smaller plates. Whether the plate he was inserting into the stack was bigger or smaller is irrelevant: it will be automatically in a place that doesn't mix the two different sizes of plate. This is how you can sort the two sizes of plate without inspecting the plate you are inserting into the pile.

5
Clues to Solve?

Mrs Hudson did it this way: CLUES, FLUES, FLOES, SLOES, SLOTS, SLATS, SLAVS, SLAVE, SOAVE, SOLVE.

The question is, can you do it in fewer moves?

6
Cryptic Clues

(a) Marylebone (anagram of 'loner may be')

(b) Laptops (spot, pal reversed = lap + tops)

(c) The Tong (anagram of 'To Ghent')

(d) Petri dishes (anagram of 'pith resides')

7
Grand Theft Automated

No, it's not possible. To work that trick, the drink would have to be transparent so the searchers wouldn't think to empty it out as they could see through it anyway. But to get a diamond to disappear in it, you'd need to match the refractive indices of the diamond and the liquid, which commits you to putting it into something such as baby oil – a method occasionally used by diamond smugglers, but not a suitable drink at a bar. Of course, among the ice at the bottom of a glass it might be hard to spot, but the searchers would have been aware of that possibility and checked that. So, however it was hidden, it wasn't like that. Perhaps the thief swallowed it.

8

Trouble with Nils

£1,953,637.

10 can be written as 2 x 5; and 1,000,000,000 can be written as 10^9 or more usefully $(2 \times 5)^9 = (2)^9 \times (5)^9$. That is just a shorthand way of writing a short billion as (2 x 2 x 2 x 2 x 2 x 2 x 2 x 2 x 2) x (5 x 5 x 5 x 5 x 5 x 5 x 5 x 5 x 5).

Now to recover the two numbers that Nils multiplied together, we want to split these 18 prime factors into two sets: one belonging to the first number and one belonging to the second. There are so many ways of doing this: (2) x (2 x 2 x 2 x 2 x 2 x 2 x 2 x 2 x 5 x 5 x 5 x 5 x 5 x 5 x 5 x 5 x 5); or (2 x 2 x 2 x 5) x (2 x 2 x 2 x 2 x 2 x 2 x 5 x 5 x 5 x 5 x 5 x 5 x 5 x 5). (How many different ways are there of doing it?)

We know that neither number contained a zero. But whenever you combine a 2 and a 5 in a number by multiplication you are bound to get a 0. That is what happens when you multiply a 5 by an even number; so the only way to do this is to keep the 2s in one number and the 5s in the other. We see that one of Nils's numbers must have been (2 x 2 x 2 x 2 x 2 x 2 x 2 x 2 x 2) = 512; and the other must have been (5 x 5 x 5 x 5 x 5 x 5 x 5 x 5 x 5) = 1,953,125. The sum of these is: £1,953,637 – just shy of 2 million.

9
Rebus

(The International) Date Line

10
The Mystery of Sebastian's Watch

No, John is wrong. If you circumnavigate the globe from east to west, you need to set your watch back one hour for every 15° of longitude crossed, and you will gain 24 hours for one round trip from east to west if you don't compensate by setting your clock forward one day when you cross the International Date Line. In contrast, a west-to-east circumnavigation of the globe loses you an hour for every 15° of longitude crossed but you gain a day when you cross the Date Line. On crossing it in either direction, the calendar *date* is adjusted by one day. That doesn't mean if you nip round twice you end up being two days out. So why Sebastian's watch is two days out is indeed mysterious. Perhaps the most that can be deduced is that Sebastian had indeed crossed the Date Line twice; each time he ritualistically changed the date on his watch but rarely needed to consult the date when not flying.

11
Rebus

A–Z

I2
The East of London

CHINATOWN

I3
At the Circus

If you walk on a ball, or a cylindrical log, in order to move forwards you need to walk backwards, and vice versa.

I4
A Playful Number

These are the Suzhou symbols for 243.

I5
The Sands of Time

1.5, 1.75, 2.25 and 2.5 kilos.

Let the four weights be in increasing order: a, $a + x$, $a + x + y$, and $a + x + y + z$.

Then the pairwise combinations are: $2a + x$, $2a + x + y$, $2a + 2x + y$, $2a + x + y + z$, $2a + 2x + y + z$ and $2a + 2x + 2y + z$. These can all be placed in an unambiguous order apart from the middle two. These must be the two pairwise readings that have the same value. That means that $x = z$.

The second reading exceeds the first by y, so $y = 3.75 - 3.25 = 0.5$. The middle reading exceeds the second by x; so $x = 4 - 3.75 = 0.25$. From this we deduce that $a = 1.5$. With these values we can get the above values of weights.

16
A Bolt from the Blue

It's certainly not as simple as Dimmock suggests. There must be an element of skill and learning involved, and that will skew things a little. But if it were completely random, his third shot was just as likely to be worse as better. (Imagine you want to flip a coin three times and get three heads; you get heads on both the first two goes; that doesn't mean the third go is more likely to be a head than a tail. It remains stubbornly at 1/2. That's because you don't 'get any better' at flipping a coin.) Furthermore, the probability of getting the third shot inside the first two might be significantly lower than the probability of hitting the target as far away as they are. So Dimmock's argument does not apply.

17
Intrusive Thoughts

Bear Cub and Gorilla.

18
From John's Blog

Let's go through the coins in decreasing order of worth. He can't have had a pound coin; or he'd have been able to give a pound. He can have at most one 50p piece, or he'd have a pound. He can have no more than four 20p pieces (since five would make a pound). No subset of these will combine with the 50p to make a pound. He can't have any 10p pieces (because one 10p would combine with the 50p and two 20p pieces to make a pound). He can have one 5p piece and four 2p pieces. But he can't have any penny coins, as just one would combine with the 2p coins and the 5p piece to make the 10p needed for the exact pound.

That makes: 50p + 20p + 20p + 20p + 20p + 5p + 2 p + 2p + 2p + 2p = £1.43 in all. This is the most John could have had without being able to give exactly £1 to the homeless man.

19
Acrostic

C l u e **S**

R o m a n t i **C**

I c **E**

M o r o **N**

E y **E**

THE
GREAT
GAME

I
Cryptic Clue

Ostentatious access road – or storage device (5, 5)

2
Mycroft's Problem

Mycroft was clearly exercised about the loss of the memory stick containing details of the Bruce-Partington Project. 'It will look exactly like this one – which contains the plans for the submarine to launch it from,' he told his visitor.

John studied the logo on the proffered device. 'Snazzy two-tone,' he said.

'Not exactly a word I would ever admit to my extensive vocabulary, but I suppose it is a sentiment I can give my conditional assent to.'

An awkward silence fell. During it, can you say what fraction of the area of the logo is grey?

John's Problem

'You really could be working for us, you know that, Dr Watson, don't
you? It can't be easy working with my little brother – he's so... chaotic.'
Mycroft removed a paper from his desk and turned it towards John.
'You've heard of magic squares, John? You just have to fill in the
squares so that the sum of the three numbers in each row, column and
the two diagonals comes to the same total.'

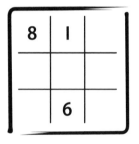

John recoiled. 'What is this, a test?'

'Just a playful challenge. Nothing hangs on it.'

John could see that there was a long way round the problem; Sherlock
would call it the dull, plodding way, he thought. Were his arithmetic
skills up to it? He was a bit rusty. Could he stay awake long enough to
do it? And then he saw that there was an easy, aesthetic way of doing it
that used his special skill.

What were the two ways?

4
A Job Offer

'Superb, John. My little brother may overlook them, but I've always relished your little glimmers of intelligence. And I'm sure you must be tired of applauding his most elementary deductions. Why not take a look at some of our intelligence tests? So much more inspiring than the dull questions you would be asked if you applied to GCHQ. We value creativity here, you see. Creative thinking, creative accounting. Creative anything, really. Take your time. There are a couple of things I need to see to.'

Mycroft slid a file over to John and slipped smoothly out of the room. With a sigh, John picked the file up and began to read...

a. Is this a good question?

b. Put one mathematical symbol between 1 and 2 to produce a number between 1 and 2.

c. How many times can you subtract 3 from 13?

d. Draw three identical squares in such a way that it produces as many squares as possible.

e. What two-digit number is reduced by 42 when you turn it upside-down?

f. What number is 15 less when you turn it upside-down?

g. The runner who was seven places in front of the runner who came in second to last came in four places ahead of the runner who came in eleventh. How many runners were there in the race?

h. You roll a number of dice; the chances of all of them scoring 3 are the same as the chances of none of them scoring 3. How many dice?

i. Cut the square shown into three pieces; two of the pieces should be identical. Rearrange them to make an arrow pointing to the right.

j. A reciprocal is one over a whole number; so the reciprocal of 7 is 1/7. This concerns the reciprocals of three different digits. One reciprocal divided by another gives a third. Which reciprocals? Give the best answer.

k. Which is larger: $1/(3 - \sqrt{8})$ or $3 + \sqrt{8}$?

l. You have an urn with two white balls in and another identical-looking urn with a white ball and a black ball in. You reach in and pull out a ball; it is white. What is the probability the other ball is black?

m. Prove that you can make any whole number apart from 1 by adding a suitable number of 2s and/or 3s together.

n. You are told there is a three-digit number beginning with 7 which is a multiple of 9. You are told the last digit. Still you cannot work out what it is. What are the two possibilities?

o. Can you cover a 10 x 10 grid as shown with T shapes of the type shown — without gaps or overlap?

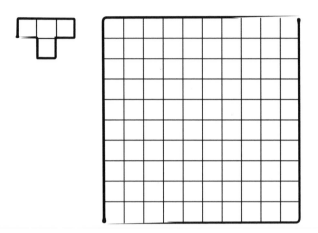

p. Fred is 36 and is twice as old as Bert was when Fred was as old as Bert is now. How old is Bert?

q. M is to OK as P is to?

r. Some words that might belong in the same category as REDBEARD are:

BILLIONAIRE
HOSTAGE
WASTELAND
SUGARCOATING
MOTHERBOARD
PROGRAMMER

Can you suggest any more?

s. The only barber in the village of Beardscombe, Sam, says: 'I shave *all* and *only* the men in our town who do not shave themselves.' Is

Sam telling the truth?

t. 'Cretans always lie,' says the Cretan. What can be deduced?

u. 'Cretans always lie. I am a Cretan.' What can be deduced?

v. You are trapped in a maze with four crazy assassins. The entrance
    has been blocked off and we may assume that any encounters
    are between a pair. You all circulate and each of you is as likely to
    meet any one of the others. You are unarmed, but the assassins
    are crazy: if you meet one, he will kill you; if two assassins meet,
    they will eliminate each other. Before this game starts, you are
    made a generous offer by the cruel person who has thought
    up this game. You may reduce the number of assassins by one.
    Should you accept?

w. Rearrange the planks to form a square made from all
    five planks.

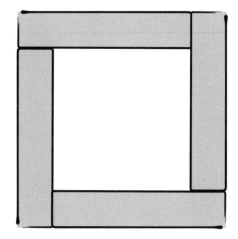

x. Which two letters could replace the asterisk?

*ELILAG

y. What letter should conclude this short sequence:

W L S C T S ?

z. You are interrogating the Apostle Gang: Matthew, Mark, Luke and John. You are allowed to interrogate one of them. The instruction as to which one to choose is hidden at the end of this paragraph. Which one should you interrogate?

5
Anagrams

(a) EVIL POST VEXES – Moriarty's idea of loud clothing? (9, 4)

(b) DRY COLA STAND – where the boys meet Lestrade (8, 4)

(c) GREAT RALLY – where Miss Wenceslas hung out (3, 7)

(d) LEVERET MOTHERS – now there's a fake! (3, 4, 7)

(e) MUSEUMS – A TAD SAD – where to see stars on the Marylebone Road? (6, 8)

(f) NONRELATIONAL DUMP – where to see stars on the Marylebone Road?(6, 11)

6
Cryptic Clues

(a) Pale bonhomie by means of which Moriarty communicates with Sherlock (1, 6, 5)

(b) Terrain providing the first clue in the game (7)

7
Quiz

What is the name of the sculpture underneath which the second hostage was found at Piccadilly Circus?

8
Two Designs

When Sherlock entered the Hickman Gallery Miss Wenceslas was looking at a design for the proposed extension to the new Töbler-One Gallery from the point of view of security cameras. It concerned itself with the latest of modern art.

Gallery floor plan

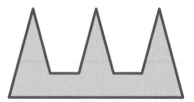

The upper part was unmodifiable but the building was to be extended downwards. The question the architect was considering was: How far downwards?

Proposed extension

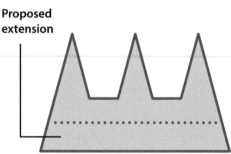

How many security guards does the first gallery need if there are to be no blind spots?

What about the second?

Can it be extended enough that only one guard is needed?

9
He's Behind You

a) In what famous London institution does the confrontation take place?

b) What is a Golem?

c) What is Sherlock's attacker's real name?

d) What is his usual MO?

e) Why did Woodbridge have to die?

SOLUTIONS

I
Cryptic Clue

Flash drive

2
Mycroft's Problem

Half.

First consider the row of five squares:

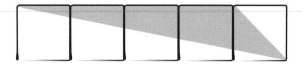

At the bottom we have 5/2 white squares (by symmetry, it's half of the row); then we need to add half a white square (top right corner). That makes three white squares. But there are six squares in the original diagram; so it's exactly half. It might seem odd to ignore part of the figure to work out the answer, but it's the quickest way.

3
John's Problem

Before Mycroft passed the paper across, John had glimpsed it upside-down. He realised that if you turned the paper the other way up it was just the bog-standard magic square that people drew whenever they showed you what a magic square looks like.

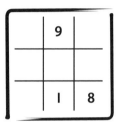

He remembered that each digit from 1 to 9 appeared once, so the middle number must be a 5. The magic number (the number each row, column and diagonal must sum to) must therefore be 9 + 5 + 1 = 15. You can then fill in the empty squares in the order of the ringed numbers 1–5 using that fact, getting the result shown.

The dull ploddy way? Assume the middle number is m; then you know the magic number is 3m. We then deduce the missing numbers one by one in the order of the ringed numbers.

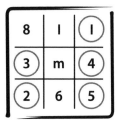

The result is:

8	1	m-2
-3	m	10
m+2	6	-1

We still don't know m; but we note that the middle column sums to m + 7; and the diagonal containing 3 undetermined numbers sums to m + 2 + m + m - 2 = 3m. But this must equal m + 7; so m + 7 = 3m, so that m = 7/2. We can then fill in the rest of the square explicitly.

8	1	3/2
-3	7/2	10
11/2	6	-1

4
A Job Offer

a. If this is a good answer.

b. 1.2 [If you put 1√2, Mycroft will account that 'correct but inelegant'. In his orderly world you get points for the neatness of your solutions!]

c. If you thought the answer was 'only once, as after that you are subtracting it from 10', mark yourself down. The correct answer is: 'As many times as you like; the correct answer will always be 10.' Accuracy matters.

d.

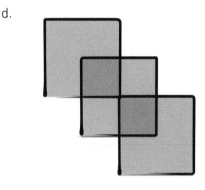

e. 42. The only invertible digits are 0, 1, 2, 5, 8 (which stay the same when viewed upside-down) and 6 and 9 (which change into each other). To get a difference ending in 2 we need to subtract 0 from 2 (not possible as one of the two-digit numbers would have to begin with 0 and that would make it a one-digit number); or subtract 6 from 8 (the numbers would then have to be 98 and 86; (the difference is 12– so that won't do); or subtract 9 from a number ending in 1; in this case the numbers would have to be 19 and 61; and the difference is indeed 42.

f.   553751. How much more difficult to do a question which looks almost the same but relies on a totally different mechanism for its solution. You start from where you left off with the last question, and that's the wrong place to start. This is a trick question, and the answer is the number 553751, as that reads 15LESS upside down.

g.   Fifteen runners. The runner who was seven places in front of the runner who came in second to last was eight places ahead of the one who came in last. If he was four places ahead of the runner who came in eleventh, he must have been in seventh place. If he was in seventh place and he was eight places ahead of the last, there must have been 7 + 8 = 15 runners.

You can also draw this out as shown below, where R is the runner, E is the runner in 11th place, P is the second-to-last runner and L is the last.

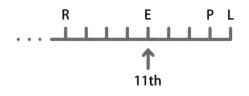

h.   Five dice. The chances that one die returns a '3' are 1/6; the chances that 4 dice do not turn up a '3' are (5/6) x (5/6) x (5/6) x (5/6); so the chances of exactly one '3' are: 5 x (1/6) x (5/6) x (5/6) x (5/6) x (5/6). (That initial 5 is because there are 5 possible choices of the die which turns up the '3'.) But the chances of no 3s are (5/6) x (5/6) x (5/6) x (5/6) x (5/6), which you will observe comes to exactly the same thing. And, yes, this is the only possible answer.

i. Cut the square shown into three pieces; two of the pieces should be identical. Rearrange them to make an arrow pointing to the right.

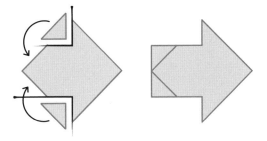

j. The possibilities are: (1/8)/(1/4) = 1/2 [and what is the same thing, rearranged: (1/8)/(1/2) = 1/4]; (1/6)/(1/2) = 1/3 [and what is the same thing rearranged: (1/6)/(1/3) = 1/2]. Of course the 'neatest' answer is (1/6)/(1/2) = 1/3, as one reciprocal divided by another equals 'a third'.

k. Neither. [For those that like the detail: If we multiply both numbers by (3 - √8), the first gives us 1; the second gives us (3 + √8)(3 - √8) = 9 - 3√8 + 3√8 - 8 =9 - 8 = 1.]

l. One third. You know there are three balls left, and only one of them is black.

m. Well, we can certainly make 2 and 3; and 4 = 2 + 2 and 5 is 2 + 3; and 6 = either 2 + 2 + 2 or 3 + 3. If some numbers bigger than 5 cannot be made in that way there must be a first one that can't. Call the number before that 'N'. Now N consists of either:

- a sum of just 2s;
- a sum of 3s and at least one 2;
- or a sum of just 3s.

In the first two cases replace one 2 by a 3. That will give you the next number, N + 1. But then the next number after N is makeable with just 2s and 3s. In the third case – the number is made by summing just 3s – replace a 3 with two 2s and we get the next number. Either way, given any number after 6 that can be made by summing 2s and 3s, we can always make the next. And so, any whole number more than 5 can be made in this way.

n. It can only be 702 or 792. There is only one possibility for every third digit other than 2.

o. No. Imagine we have achieved the desired result and we have a 10 x 10 grid made up of 100/4 = 25 Tees. Colour the squares black and white like a chessboard. Clearly half the little squares will be black and half will be white. Now cut that finished grid into these 25 Tee shapes. Any Tee shape must have either 3 white squares and one black (mostly white); or 3 black squares and one white (mostly black); so the only way of having the same total of white squares and black squares is if there are the same number of mostly black pieces as mostly white pieces. But the number of Tee shapes is odd. So the answer is: no, you can't.

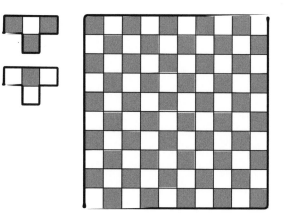

p. 27. [If Bert is b years old, then when Fred was b, it was 36 − b years ago. Bert's age 36 − b years ago was b − (36 − b) = 2b − 36. But 36 is twice this age, so 36 = 2(2b − 36); that is 18 = 2b − 36; solving for b, we find b = 27. Checking: when Fred was 27 was 9 years ago; 9 years ago Bert was 27 − 9 = 18. And Fred's age now (36) is indeed twice 18.]

q. L or N. ['M is to OK' = MISTOOK; to make a word from 'P is to −' we could try PISTON or PISTOL.]

r. REDBEARD conceals an animal: BEAR (redBEARd); we have also: milLIONnaire; hoSTAGe; wastELAND; sugarCOATIng; motherBOARd; progRAMmer; so any word concealing an animal. wRATh would do.

s. If Sam is a man, he is lying: if he didn't shave himself, he *would* shave himself; if he *did* shave himself, he wouldn't shave himself. So Sam is either a lying man, or a woman (who might or might not be lying).

t. He cannot be a Cretan if what he says is true as he'd have to be lying; and if he was lying then not all Cretans are liars. We conclude he is a Cretan and he is lying when he says all Cretans lie (no paradox there!); or I lied when I said that he was a Cretan. But if I was lying all bets are off anyway.

u. Either the speaker is a Cretan and lying in the first statement but telling the truth in the second; or telling the truth in the first statement but lying in the second; or both statements are false. All these are possible. What is impossible is that both statements be true!

v. No. If there are three assassins, then even if two of them meet and eliminate each other there will be one unbalanced assassin left over who will definitely finish you off; if there are four, there is always the chance that all four will eliminate each other; so you are better off with four mad assassins than just three under the conditions of this game!

Point to Ponder: Your chances of survival are 0 if there are three assassins; what are your chances of survival if there are four?

w.

x. A or O (depending on whether it is read GALILEA or GALILEO when read from back to front).

y. S. [These are the initial letters of the question.]

z. Mark. [The paragraph ends in '?' = 'Question Mark.']

5
Anagrams

(a) EXPLOSIVE VEST

(b) SCOTLAND YARD

(c) ART GALLERY

(d) THE LOST VERMEER

(e) MADAME TUSSAUDS

(f) LONDON PLANETARIUM

6
Cryptic

(a) A mobile phone

(b) Trainer

7
Quiz

Most people think it is Eros. In fact the sculptor sculpted it as Anteros (Eros's brother and the god of unrequited love).

8
Two Designs

The first diagram can manage with 3 security guards (or security cameras).

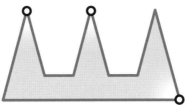

In the second design we can make do with just two.

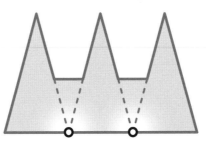

If the extension is extended far enough downwards we can manage with just one guard. But that would be going to 'ridiculous lengths'.

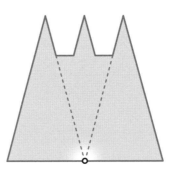

9
He's Behind You

(a) The London Planetarium on the Marylebone Road

(b) In Jewish folklore, a creature made from clay or mud and brought
to life by a magic ritual; he could not speak and did his animator's
bidding. A fitting nickname in this case. The most famous was the
Golem of Prague.

(c) Oscar Dzundza – a Czech

(d) He strangles his victims with his bare hands.

(e) He was an amateur astronomer and had spotted an astronomical
detail in the Vermeer which meant it must be
a fake.

A SCANDAL IN BELGRAVIA

I
The Language of Flowers

'Sherlock, you've got a secret admirer!' declared Mrs Hudson as she brought up the bouquet delivered to the door of 221B Baker Street. 'But he was such a nice young man! Very polite, very respectful. Mind you, odd sort of bouquet, if you ask me: it's only got two irises, a daffodil, a tulip and an orchid. Ooh, and there's a card, look – it's just signed "W". Another little mystery for you, dear.'

Sherlock leapt up from the couch. 'Mrs Hudson!' he exclaimed. 'Your powers of deduction are even more pitiful than John's. It's not a gift, it's an insult. And this little bunch of spite comes from someone beginning with an "M".'

He snatched the flowers and threw them at the overflowing wastepaper bin, where they perched awkwardly. Mrs Hudson watched him with an air of reproach and bewilderment.

What was the message?

2
Conditional Knowledge

'What is it?' asked Sherlock.

'What's what?'

'What is it that you don't want me to see in the newspaper you hid behind your back as soon as you heard me coming up the stairs?'

'How did...? Oh, never mind.' John handed Sherlock the *Standard*.

'Thank you. Now... Puzzles? A puzzle page. Are you trying to exercise your... Oh, God. This is because of your damn blog, isn't it?'

'Sorry. They do say imitation is the best form of flattery.'

'I don't need flattering. Anyone praising me is either stating the obvious or underlining his own good taste.'

'Oh really? Sherlock, you love praise. Remember when you asked that angler what he was fishing for? He said, "Carp, mate, and what are you fishing for?" And you replied, "Compliments". I might send that one in to the paper, actually.'

'Don't you dare! Let's see this puzzle. "The planet Blotto orbits its sun in four years; the planet Speedo in three years. At the moment the planets and the sun all lie in the same straight line. When will all three celestial bodies once more lie in a straight line?" Easy. Boring and easy.'

'You don't need me to explain "orbit" to you, then?'

3

Fakery

Sherlock wrenched open the door to his room and spoke sharply to the blonde woman standing there: 'Hello – I'm looking for a case; something with a bit of zing. Does your problem have that special something?'

'I'm a herpetologist,' the woman explained. 'I study snakes.'

'Yes, we know what a herpetologist is.'

'From the Greek for "creep",' offered John. 'How can we help?' He smiled hopefully at the woman.

'Don't worry about John,' muttered Sherlock. 'He's got a thing about freckles.'

'I've lost a snake. It's a boa constrictor.' She smiled back at John. 'Unless you'd prefer its Latin name?'

'Nonsense,' snapped Sherlock. 'You're no more a herpetologist than John here. What do you *really* want?'

The smile faded from their visitor's face. 'Ah. OK. What gave me away?'

Well – what had?

4
A Wild Surmise

'I do wish you'd answer your own door occasionally, Sherlock,' complained Mrs Hudson.

'So do I, Mrs Hudson, so do I!' replied Sherlock. 'But it's too late now, so why not tell us who it is?'

'He mumbled something about Jersey, but he's got a funny accent. European. Maybe you have his jumper or something?' ventured their landlady.

'Ah, he must be Polish, then,' concluded Sherlock.

'Go on, then,' sighed John. 'Dazzle us with your brilliance.'

'Oh, come on, John. It's just a question of probabilities.' He glanced up as their visitor walked into the room. '*Dzien dobry*. And why did you get rid of the beard? I think it would have suited you.'

'It was annoying in this heat,' said the newcomer. 'But how did you know that?'

How *did* he know?

5
Same Difference

Identify the two places which are spelt the same apart from the letters shown:

H******* (Where Sherlock goes to meet Mycroft)

D**** *** (Frank Hudson's last accommodation)

6
Dead Reckoning

With Mycroft attending to another matter, his staff loaded the bodies onto the jumbo jet at Heathrow, and they made a dog's dinner of it. Every dead passenger had been labelled with his or her seat number, but when they carried the first corpse onto the plane they discovered his label was missing. Rather stupidly, in hindsight, they picked a seat number at random and put him there.

They then brought up the other 'passengers'. If the seat corresponding to their label was free, that's where they went; if the seat was taken, rather than juggling bodies they chose another free seat at random, one by one.

Prove that the last body brought up would either find the correct seat free, or that of the first unlabelled body – each with a probability of 1/2.

7
Enigma

Does Irene Adler like champagne?

8
Quiz

(a) What does Mycroft mean by 'the Coventry Conundrum'?

(b) What does *Adler* mean in German?

(c) What was Irene Adler's Twitter handle?

(d) What was Adler's safe number?

(e) What number did Sherlock key in to access Adler's phone?

9
Cryptic Clues

(a) What Irene might have told herself on a scale of 1–10 – and what Sherlock was (6)

(b) Swap rods around – it's necessary to gain access to Adler's phone? (8)

IO
The Pantless Visit

The newspaper seller stared at the two giggling men.

'Looks like the papers have heard about our Palace visit,' said the shorter one. 'Perhaps Mycroft's been *debriefed*.'

'The *naked cheek* of it!' said the one with the hair.

'"Sherlock, what *are* you doing?"' said the first in a high-pitched voice, then dropped a tone: '"Oh, nothing, brother dear – just *hanging out*."'

The pair fell about. Then the one with the hair wiped a tear from his eye and said, 'I might pick up a copy.'

'But it's a tabloid. Don't you need... a *broad sheet*?'

'I like the headline,' wheezed the taller man between giggles. 'It's quite clever for once.'

'Yes,' snorted his friend. 'They're usually... *pants*!'

As the two men roared, the vendor looked down at the front page:

QUEEN LEFT IN SHOCK BY DETECTIVE

For the life of him, he couldn't see what was so clever about it.

Can you?

There was a ping, and Sherlock scrutinised his smartphone. 'Clearly not everyone is a fan,' he remarked and handed it to John. The text read:

'It seems to be about a meeting of some sort, between someone called Friedrich and Brigadier Mattock,' ventured John.

'So why was it sent to me?' said Sherlock.

'By mistake?'

'Oh, it's no mistake,' said Sherlock. He took the phone back and rearranged the words into a stack:

Back

Friedrich

Wednesday

Brigadier

Mattock

Archway

Send

'I think it's the *beginning* of something. And –' he jumped up and gave a little whoop – 'the *middle*! And the *end* – in Archway, of all places!'

'So we're going to Archway, are we?' asked John uncertainly.

'No, John,' laughed Sherlock. 'I have a fan – but what sort depends on whether this message is just a statement or a threat.'

What was the message?

12
Mycroft

(a) What was Mycroft's harmless remark that evoked a reproachable barb from Sherlock?

(b) What was the task that caused Mycroft to have Sherlock brought to the Palace?

(c) Of what is the equerry's employer a tremendous fan?

(d) What did Mycroft give Sherlock at Christmas on seeing he was sad to think Adler was dead?

(e) What language did Mycroft claim to have mastered in a couple of hours?

13
Is It Me or Is It Hot in Here?

(a) What does Irene Adler have gripped between her teeth?

(b) Why is Watson holding a bowl?

(c) What trick do the duo use to locate Adler's safe?

(d) What reappeared mysteriously as Sherlock regained consciousness from the injection Adler gave him in 221B?

SOLUTIONS

I

The Language of Flowers

The initials of the flowers listed by Mrs Hudson are IIDTO. As Sherlock put it: 'You don't imagine they stood for "I DO IT", do you? No, it can only be "IDIOT".'

'You must be very upset,' deadpanned John.

'Oh yes, heartbroken. He doesn't believe it's true or he wouldn't have sent it. No, it's meant to wind me up. But the fact that he spends his time on this pettiness tells me that my existence gets to him, because he knows I am the one thing that can stop him. So in a backhanded sort of way, it's a compliment. Oh – and a threat.'

'A threat?'

'Well, yes. "I know where you live."'

2
Conditional Knowledge

In six years' time, the planet Blotto will have made one and a half orbits, while Speedo will have managed two orbits. All three celestial bodies will once again be in a straight line, though not in the same order.

3
Fakery

The (Latin) scientific name for the boa constrictor is *Boa constrictor*, as any herpetologist would know.

4
A Wild Surmise

The visitor's name was Jerzy. Since coming to London, Jerzy had tried to get people to say his name with the correct pronunciation but had finally given up and gone with the flow. As for the beard, because he had shaved when the weather became hot, the shaved part was detectibly lighter than the slight tan of the rest of the face.

5
Same Difference

HEATHROW, DEATH ROW.

6
Dead Reckoning

Consider the last person to be brought aboard. Each body brought on board after the first occupied either their own seat or another if their own was already occupied. So the only possibilities for vacant seats are the unlabelled person's seat or the last passenger's.

Suppose the unlabelled body's proper seat is U and the last person's proper seat is L. Now suppose we have placed the unlabelled one in a random seat. When we bring up a person who is labelled with that seat number, instead of taking that passenger to another random seat, we move the unlabelled one to another random seat; this will have no effect whatsoever on which seats are empty and which are occupied.

Now at each stage we are only interested in the relative probabilities that the unlabelled one ends up in U or L. But since at each stage there is nothing to choose between these, by symmetry the probability he occupies U is the same as the probability he occupies L; what's more if he takes up U he can rest in peace; and if he ends up in L he will be undisturbed until L gets on. So – for the whole of the process between the unlabelled one and the last one being brought on board – the probabilities that the unlabelled man occupies U or L are equal; but these are the only two possibilities.

So the probability the unlabelled man ends up in his own seat are 1/2 (in which case the last body boarding's seat will be free); and the chances of the unlabelled man occupying L's seat are also 1/2; so the chances that when the last body gets aboard his seat is taken are 1/2.

7
Enigma

No, she prefers the real thing.

8
Quiz

(a) The term 'Coventry Conundrum' is sometimes used to describe the dilemma of intelligence analysts who know that if they take action on information secretly obtained it might reveal that they have access to the enemy's messages. The term supposedly arose from an incident during the Second World War, when British intelligence learned of German plans for an air raid on Coventry. If they had warned Coventry, the Germans would suspect the British knew in advance and they would then realise the British had cracked the Enigma code. If the Germans had then changed to a different system of coding, it would have been a severe blow to the allies' war effort. The story goes that Intelligence did not warn Coventry and so kept the cracking of the Enigma code a secret from the Germans.

(b) Eagle.

(c) @TheWhipHand

(d) 32-24-34

(e) 7-4-3-7

9
Cryptic Clues

(a) Beaten (be a ten)

(b) Password

IO
The Pantless Visit

Queen = ER; left = L. Put these in 'SHOCK' and you get 'SHERLOCK'.

II
Post Mortem

Sherlock spotted that there was something awkward about the words of the message that didn't quite ring true. And why had it been sent to him? These intuitions were confirmed when he spotted that the middle letter of each one taken in turn spelt out a word:

Frie**d**rich

Wedn**e**sday

Brig**a**dier

Mat**t**ock

Arc**h**way

Now, the chances that five words chosen at random (i.e. chosen without regard for their length) should all have an odd number of letters would be about 3 per cent. But when you consider, on top of that, that those letters, in order, make a word, the chances are tiny. So it was almost certainly a threat.

12
Mycroft

(a) 'I'll be mother.' To which Sherlock replied, 'Our childhood in a nutshell.' No wonder Mycroft gave him that dirty look.

(b) To get hold of Irene Adler's smartphone.

(c) John's blog

(d) A cigarette

(e) Serbian. Presumably it would have taken even longer if it hadn't had a Slavic root.

13
Is It Me or Is It Hot in Here?

(a) Sherlock's fake dog collar

(b) To bathe Sherlock's cut

(c) They set off the fire alarm

(d) His coat (used to cover Adler's nudity); she also added her number to his phone, and added an erotic ringtone

THE
HOUNDS OF
BASKERVILLE

I
Dire Warnings

Before Sherlock and John set off for the Moors, a courier arrived with no fewer than four messages.

'Better than buses,' remarked Sherlock. He opened them and laid them on the table:

Stay away from Baskerville

Keep away from the Moors

The premises are guarded by dogs!

See Devon and die, Consulting Defective

'Nothing interesting here. One is from someone with no taste. One is a bit of a boaster. Oh, ha, ha – "Consulting Defective"? Moriarty, although the Georgian connection escapes me. But I think the other one might just be a friendly warning from someone within the establishment itself.'

'How do you do that?' asked Watson.

'Easy,' replied Sherlock, 'just be me.'

'Now who's boasting?'

Which message did he think might be a friendly warning and why?

2
The Pub on the Moors

'So what brings you all the way down to the Moors?' John asked the two tourists.

'Oh, just the hunt,' they told him.

'I thought that sort of thing had been banned.'

'Oh, John,' interjected Sherlock. 'Don't embarrass us in front of our *gifted visitors*. And if the accent has misled you, it's not north, but east.'

Where were the tourists from, and what had they come for?

3
A Slight Check

There are three guards at the end of the corridor blocking their progress. Above the door they need to go through, it says, 'Smullyan Wing: Let no one ignorant of logic enter here.'

Armed with information stolen from Mycroft, Sherlock knows the guards are Andy, Bandy and Candy. He can only pass if he identifies one of them correctly. He is allowed only two questions, and they are allowed to answer only yes or no. Andy always tells the truth. Bandy alternates: he answers one question with a lie and the next one with the truth (or is it the other way around?). Candy always lies.

'It's no use asking, "Is that Andy?"' ponders John. 'You don't know if your answer is true or a lie.'

'Wrong question, John!' said Sherlock.

He went up to one of them and asked two questions. What might they have been?

4
The Hunter Hunted

In the grid shown, A represents the dread hound and you are B. You each take it in turns and A moves first. Each move consists of going to the next intersection. If A arrives at the same intersection as B, A has caught B – that is, the Hound has got you! (If you are of a sensitive disposition you can pretend B is a luminous rabbit escaped from the labs and you – in the role of A – just want to recapture it humanely.)

Show that if no one may visit X, capture is always possible. What happens if X may be visited?

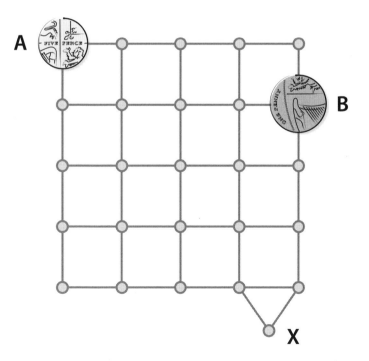

5
A Message from Moriarty

As they prepared to return to Baker Street, there was a ping and Sherlock looked down at the text arriving on his phone. This time it was just a stack of words without any pretence of meaning:

TREBLE
BARNET
MARY
LARD
BEDS
SHED
MEAL
TIDING

'Perhaps they're anagrams,' John wondered. 'I mean, MARY makes ARMY.'

'Yes... and then MEAL would be – LAME! No, it's undoubtedly to do with the middle letters.'

'OK, so... Sherlock, they don't *have* middle letters.'

'Exactly!' countered Sherlock. 'So we must find them.'

What was the hidden message?

6
Rebus

What Moriarty was to Sherlock (9)

7
Your Place or Mine

Lestrade picked up a tattered and charred piece of paper. 'Crib sheet,' he said, showing it to them. 'He must have been making a bolt for home and was in too much of a hurry to use it.'

They contemplated Frankland's body, which lay broken at the heart of the Grimpen minefield.

'It shows a grid, and the number of mines in each column and row are given. Clearly 1–6 each appear once and once only along the top and along the side.'

'But some figures are missing,' objected John.

'Lucky us, then,' remarked Sherlock. 'Frankland was kind enough to leave us something useful. *Even in death, I still serve.*'

'It's just a game to you, isn't it,' complained Lestrade.

'Yes. Fun, isn't it?'

Can you reconstruct Frankland's crib sheet?

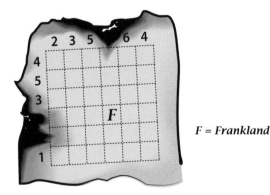

F = Frankland

8
It's a Gas

John dreams he is back in the laboratories at Baskerville. Before him are a number of identical-looking cylinders. Seven contain oxygen, five contain hallucinogen, and three contain an antidote to the hallucinogen. If you take the antidote *before* being exposed to the hallucinogen, you are immune to the hallucinogen for an hour or so. John starts to open the cylinders one by one and at random. What are the chances he'll be able to release all the gas without any ill effects from the hallucinogen some of them contain? Hurry, there is the hiss of leaking gas somewhere nearby.

9
Quiz

(a) What was the name of the pub the duo stayed in? (3, 5, 4)

(b) What were the names of the owners? (4 and 5)

(c) Where did Henry experience his original apparition? (6, 6)

10
Cryptic Clues

(a) They might change your ideas about Dartmoor – and badly unhinge locals (13)

(b) Bad mistake in deduction – or a hound on the prowl? (6)

(c) Henry's therapist found in outlier's memoir (6, 8)

SOLUTIONS

I

Dire Warnings

Sherlock was reacting to the fonts. The first message was in a font called 'Baskerville'. He is less then enamoured of 'the joyous inanity that is Comic Sans'. Moriarty's is in the font named 'Georgia'. The heavy one is in 'Braggadocio'. Sherlock's remarks were really about the fonts, but Watson took them to be about the senders.

2

The Pub on the Moors

They were Germans, hence Sherlock's little 'gifted' reference, harking back to his fridge magnets puzzle. Terminal 'd' is pronounced as 't' in German, so they had come because of 'der Hund', not for 'the hunt'. The deep way the Germans had pronounced the 'u' had tripped John into thinking he'd heard a northern English accent; as Sherlock remarked, 'Once you have made a false step it's hard to retract it and get to the obvious conclusion.'

3

A Slight Check

Sherlock just chose one of them at random and asked 'Are you Bandy?' twice. If the guard answered 'Yes' to both questions he was clearly Candy; if he answered 'No' to both questions he was clearly Andy; only if he answered 'Yes' and then 'No' or vice versa could you be sure that was Bandy.

'Why didn't you go by appearance?' asked Watson as they passed through to the inner sanctum. 'Nothing in the conditions I got from Mycroft – his security is appallingly slack – said that the Candy had to be a woman.'

4

The Hunter Hunted

First colour the intersections black and white. It is possible to do this in such a way that every white vertex is connected to a black vertex and every black vertex is connected to a white one. If you both start on the same colour, the hunter cannot possibly catch you, as he goes first, so he will always be moving onto a colour opposite to the one you are on! If you start off on opposite colours, it becomes logically possible (though he might have to chase you into a corner to make good on that possibility). It follows that if you both start on different colours (as shown in the question), you need to avail yourself of the little layby at X which enables you to skip a beat and stay on the same colour for one move. Think of this as a fresh start to the game but this time one in which you both start on the same colours. The Hound now cannot catch you, unless he uses the same trick to reset the game again.

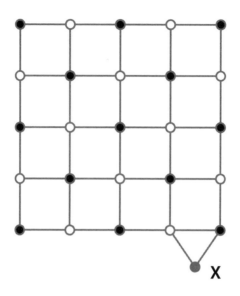

5

A Message from Moriarty

Sherlock tried adding a letter at the middle of each word – in each case making a valid word – and ended up with the stack shown here. If you line up the centres and read down you get a name:

TREM**B**LE

BAR**O**NET

MA**R**RY

LA**I**RD

BE**A**DS

SHR**E**D

ME**T**AL

TID**Y**ING

6

Rebus

Tormentor [A TOR, some MEN, and another TOR]

7

Your Place or Mine

First, the * must be a 1 (PIC A), and that must be the one Frankland trod on. So we can fill in the rest of that column with blanks. We can also fill in the column with the 6 on top, as each of those squares must have a mine in. So then we know the row with one mine is all blank apart from the mine in the column with 6 (PIC B).

We can also fill in the column with 5 in it and also the row with 5 in it. That brings us to PIC C.

Look at the two rows marked with arrows. One of them must have 6 mines in and one of them just 2. The lower one can't have 6, as there is a blank. So the upper has 6, and we can fill in all the squares in the row. The other has two in it, and they are already marked, so the rest of that row must be blank. That gets us to PIC D.

The column with 4 in it can be completed now, so also the column with 2 in it. That brings us to PIC E. The row with 3 in it needs filling in completely with blanks as we have already located the 3 mines and we have only one option for the last mine in the row with 4 in it.

This leads us to the completed grid as in PIC F.

When John and Greg looked up to say they'd worked it out, they were astonished to see Sherlock was already in the minefield and examining Frankland's inert form.

'How did you do that?'

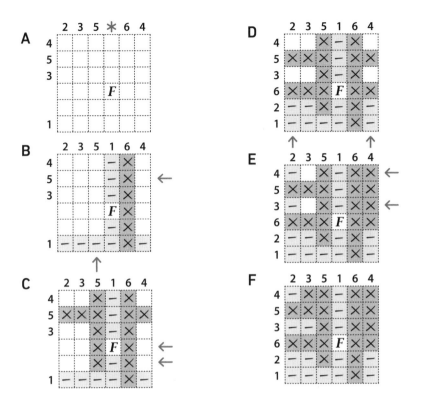

'Oh, come on – I was safe walking to where Frankland had got to or he wouldn't have got that far. And he very kindly rendered this spot safe by treading on the mine underneath it.'

'Just one thing,' said Greg. 'There doesn't seem to be a clear path through the minefield, even if you zig-zag.'

'Well done, Gary! Well, you were supposed to choose the row or column with just one mine in it and jump over that square. Frankland must have thought he was going west when he was actually going north. So I suppose you could say he went west after all.'

'Not appropriate,' said John.

8
It's a Gas

The first useful thing to note is that the oxygen cylinders are irrelevant to our calculation. All that matters is how probable it is that, in a random linear arrangement of the other eight cylinders, the first one will contain the antidote, and not the hallucinogen. Imagine withdrawing one cylinder from these eight. The chances the first one you withdraw is an antidote are 3/8, so these are John's chances of releasing all the gas without any ill effects.

9
Quiz

(a) The Cross Keys

(b) Gary and Billy

(c) Dewer's Hollow

IO
Cryptic Clues

(a) Hallucinogens

(b) Howler (double meaning)

(c) Louise Mortimer

THE
REICHENBACH
FALL

I
Fairy Tale

A legend enthrals (6, 3, 6)

2
Hansel's Sweets

The following arrived in the Forum on Sherlock's *Science of Deduction* website:

'Hansel and Gretel are blue. Hansel has some sweets in a bag: some are red; the rest are blue. The chances Gretel will choose two at random and find they're both blue are a fifth. If there are eight red sweets, how many are blue?'

Well?

3
Cryptic Clues

(a) Enliven plot with prison? (11)

(b) Where Moriarty struck at two and three – roughly? (3, 5)

(c) Where cash is kept from a TV sleuth? (3, 6)

(d) Ruminant does rabbit – on your head be it! (11)

4
A Poisonous Proposal

When Moriarty is freed, Sherlock knows a showdown is looming, and he rehearses various scenarios in his Mind Palace. In one, Moriarty challenges him to a little game.

'Take it away, Sherlock!' He places thirteen mushrooms in three heaps on the table.

'We take it in turns,' continues Moriarty, 'to remove a mushroom or mushrooms from any one of the heaps here. This mushroom here, the one with the sweaty white spots, is as poisonous as it looks. If the poisonous one is left, the person whose go it is gets to eat it all up, yum, yum! So... who's going first?'

Should Sherlock go first – or second? And what should his strategy be?

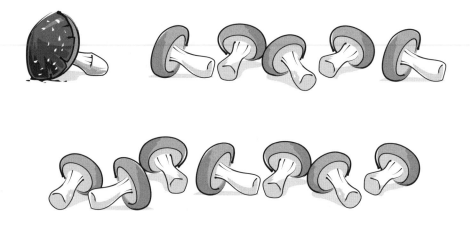

5
Have Your Cake and Eat It

'That was clever,' beamed Moriarty. 'Well done, Sherl. Let's play some more. "Have Your Cake and Eat It"?'

'Stupid saying,' scoffed Sherlock. 'What's the point of having your cake if you can't eat it?'

'Focus on the game, Sherlock Holmes,' growled Moriarty. 'I've sliced the cake into five rows and five columns. Oh, look, they're almost touching – sweet.'

'You've brought us cake – that's what's almost touching!'

'Oh, please. I've injected just one piece – the one that looks a bit different – with an entomopathogenic fungus. To eat it would be to condemn yourself to A Living Death. Ooh. Spooky!'

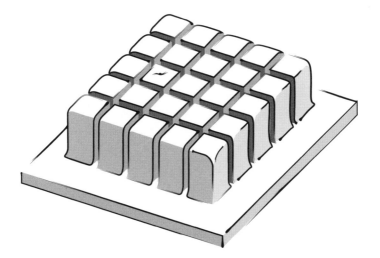

'Nope. Dull,' yawned Sherlock. 'Being born has already condemned me to a living death.'

'Now you're just being mean, Sherlock. The fungus will speed things up a bit. This time a player has to remove and gobble up either a whole number of connected rows or a whole number of connected columns on any move. One of us ends up with the poisonous piece, and whoever it is – and I'll tell you now, I'm kind of planning that it'll be you – has to eat it all up, guzzle, guzzle, choke, choke, urgh. And then perish, very slowly and ever so unpleasantly. Who's first this time? Do you wanna roll a dice?'

'Or die...' said Sherlock.

Should Sherlock go first this time? Or let Moriarty take the lead?

6
A Foreshadowing

How quickly everyone had turned on him. Anderson and Donovan, he could understand – they were idiots. But Gary Lestrade was a disappointment, after all the help he'd given him. So now he was down to John and Molly.

It was at such a really low point in his mood that Sherlock received from his usual troll the ominous text in code:

What did it mean?

7
Lost in Translation

Moriarty covered his tracks by translating Reichenbach as Rich Brook. Of whom were these fake names direct translations?

(a) John Brook

(b) Richard Bouquet

(c) Joe Green

(d) Claude Greenberg

(e) Dick Wainwright

8
Quiz

(a) Who painted the *Falls of the Reichenbach* that Sherlock rescued?

(b) What piece of Bach had Moriarty tapped out with his fingers?

(c) What was the connection between *La gazza ladra* and Moriarty at the Tower?

9
Enigma

Why did people believe Sherlock hadn't died in the spring?

SOLUTIONS

I
Fairy Tale

Hansel and Gretel

2
Hansel's Sweets

'The neat answer is two are blue – the kidnapped children. It's just masquerading as a maths problem. There are clearly seven blue sweets, and fifteen in all.'

'That doesn't exactly follow, does it?' cautioned John.

'No, I know it doesn't follow. But I see it in my mind's eye, like on a gigantic screen. All I have to do is look. So: the chances the first is blue are (7/15); the chances the second is blue are (6/14); the chances both are blue, then, are (7/15)(6/14) = 1/5. The chances they are both red, though is – in a similar way: (8/15)(7/14) = 4/15. The chances of a mixed pair must be double this: 8/15.'

John tried to follow the logical path. Let there be n sweets, then n - 8 are blue; the chances the first is blue are (n - 8)/n; of the second being blue are $(n - 9)/(n - 1)$; so that the chances both are blue are $(n - 8)/n$ x $(n - 9)/(n - 1) = 1/5$. This is the same as $(n - 8)(n - 9)/(n(n - 1)) = 1/5$. Now he multiplied both sides by $5n(n - 1)$, which led to a simpler equation: $5(n - 8)(n - 9) = n(n - 1)$.

'Getting there,' he thought. Then he multiplied out the brackets: $5(n^2 - 17n + 72) = n^2 - n$, which is the same as: $5n^2 - 85n + 360 = n^2 - n$. He then gathered together 'like terms' to get: $4n^2 - 84n + 360 = 0$. 'Well, we can divide everything by 4,' he thought, and arrived at: $n^2 - 21n + 90 = 0$.

He then factorised it (some things actually do stick in your head from school, he thought!) and arrived at: $(n - 15)(n - 6) = 0$. 'Two numbers multiply to give 0,' he reasoned, 'so we get either $n - 15 = 0$, so $n = 15$; or $n - 6 = 0$, in which case $n = 6$.'

He was relieved that his method led to a correct answer (a total of 15 sweets) which did work. But all that work just to reach a conclusion that Sherlock saw instinctively...

He was less happy to realise that his method produced another answer: 6 sweets! Well if 8 sweets are red, that would mean -2 would have to be blue. And a negative number of sweets seemed a bit weird. It was just that sort of weirdness that was not adequately explained at school. It didn't comfort him much that this weird answer also worked: if you have -2 blue sweets in a bag (don't interpret this, just go with the flow), the chances of withdrawing a blue sweet are $(-2/6)$; there are then -3 blue sweets in the bag; so the chances of withdrawing two sweets and finding both blue are $(-2)/6$ X $(-3)/(5) = (6)/(30) = 1/5$. In the end he decided, 'You can't have a negative number of blue sweets in a bag.' So he did what they did at school – swept the nonsensical answer under the carpet.

Point to Ponder: Why is it that a sensible question can give you two answers: one sensible and one absurd?

3
Cryptic Clues

(a) Pentonville

(b) The Tower

(c) The vaults

(d) Deerstalker

4

A Poisonous Proposal

He should go first. What Sherlock needs to ensure is that (ignoring the poisonous mushroom) he doesn't let Moriarty take the last good mushroom. The way to do this is to go first and to remove two mushrooms from the heap with seven, and this leaves the poisonous mushroom and two equal heaps.

Then, however many Moriarty removes from one of those two equal heaps, Sherlock can echo it by taking the same number from the other heap. That way it will be Moriarty that gets the poison mushroom. But on no account should Sherlock let Moriarty go first – or he'll play the same trick on him.

5

Have Your Cake And Eat It

This is another game where Sherlock should seize the initiative and make sure he makes the first move. In the first case, he must break off two columns from the right. This puts the poisoned piece in the centre.

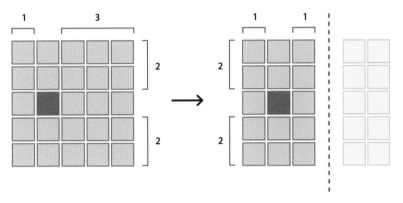

Then, whatever Moriarty does to a row or column on one side, Sherlock can match it on the other side. For every move Moriarty has, Sherlock has one to counter it. The joys of symmetry. Until, that is, Moriarty is left with the last – poisonous – piece. Rather appropriate, wouldn't you say?

Point to Ponder: What if Moriarty had infected the piece shown here instead?

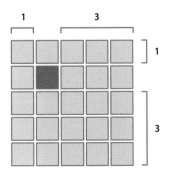

6
A Foreshadowing

If you stack it in layers of five letters, you get:

```
P   E   S   O   F
R   G   B   R   A
I   O   E   E   L
D   E   F   A   L
```

Now just read down each column in turn.

7
Lost in Translation

(a) Johann (Sebastian) Bach

(b) Richard Strauss

(c) Giuseppe Verdi

(d) Claudio Monteverdi

(e) Richard Wagner

8
Quiz

(a) J.M.W. Turner

(b) Partita No. 1 in B flat, Bach

(c) Rossini's *La gazza ladra* translates as 'The Thieving Magpie'.

9
Enigma

Because they thought he'd died in the fall.

MANY
HAPPY
RETURNS

I
Cryptic Clues

(a) Hospital togs worn by Molly Hooper's colleagues? (12)

(b) Loony vandals cruelly disparaging Sherlock (5, 7)

(c) Character dancing island hornpipe (6, 8)

2
An Obsession

Philip Anderson was convinced that Sherlock hadn't died when he fell from the roof of Barts, though how it had been done he had no idea. Or rather he had too many ideas – all wild theories and little to choose between them. He scoured the net looking for stories of weird crimes (those were the ones Sherlock had preferred) solved with powers of detection of an order that he was convinced only Sherlock could muster.

Lestrade was sure that all of this was out of guilt. 'All those times you mocked him,' he said, as they met for a drink. 'There was that case where you were convinced terrorists might be involved because you thought the Spanish guy had said "Hamas". And it was something far more banal.'

'Yes, go on, just mock,' retorted Anderson. 'Do you know what it was like playing Salieri to his bloody Mozart all the time?'

Lestrade grimaced. 'I know, I know. He made us all feel like fools at one time or another.'

And they sat musing in silence, supping their pints.

What *was* the more banal explanation?

3
Missing Presumed Less Than 5 Foot 8

'All right, all right, I admit it,' groaned Anderson. 'He was good. Like that case of the guy that disappeared and when we went to his flat we found everything terribly neat and in its place and from a tiny amount of wear and tear in the hall carpet in front of the hall mirror our wonder boy was able to predict the height of the missing occupant.'

How had he done that?

4
A Passing Observation

'I don't know how he did it,' admitted Greg. 'Things just leapt out at him. Do you remember in that other empty flat mystery, in marches Sherlock, bold as brass, goes over to the bookshelves and says, "The occupant is clearly an obsessive under 5 foot in height."'

'Well the height thing was obvious once he'd explained it.'

What was the explanation?

5

The Temple of Boom

Anderson found one foreign account on the net of a madman –
dubbed 'Artie Murray' in the press; why did that sound familiar? – who
had wired up the sixteen idols in a local temple in such a way that
they could only be defused if they were correctly removed. He had
numbered the idols 1 to 16, and they had to be removed a pair at a time
in such a way that the sum of the numbers on each pair summed to a
perfect square. Apparently, a visiting Englishman with a reversible hat
had strolled in and accomplished the task in moments. The temple had
been spared. This surely could only have been Sherlock Holmes!

In what pairs had the idols been removed?

6
Same Time, Same Place

At about the time Anderson was reading these accounts, Sherlock himself was in Tibet. He set off from the monastery before noon and arrived in the village far below in the valley in the later afternoon. He bought a few supplies and found lodgings for the night. The next day, he left at dawn and retraced the same path he had descended by, but this time the climb was so arduous and he had to stop so many times that he didn't arrive until just after sunset. Is it true – as the abbot suggested – that there must have been a point on his path where he was at the same time and place on the way up as on the way down?

7
Two Temples of Tibet

On his travels, Sherlock came across a wandering monk who spent his life making Naga Mala – necklaces to ward off evil spirits. The monk visited first one temple and then another in alternation, each time donating the same number of necklaces. Between visits, he doubled the number of these charms he had remaining. After he had visited both temples three times, he had used up all the necklaces. What was the smallest number he could have started out with? How many did he donate each visit?

8
A Crowning Achievement

In Athens, a 'tall stranger' had shown in a public demonstration that the small crown from Knossos had been stolen from the National Archaeological Museum on Patission Street and replaced with a clever fake. The original had been of a gold so pure it was almost soft; whereas this was silver, and plated with a thin layer of gold. The demonstration had taken place with a set of scales and some water. When asked how he knew, he had replied manically: 'Ask Archimedes.' This had to be him, thought Anderson. That theatricality, that really was Sherlock's kind of shtick.

How had the demonstration been made?

9
Yakuza Accuser

Then there was another case in Japan where a Yakuza boss had commissioned a gold globe from a goldsmith, identical to the one he already had. His brother had admired it and he didn't want to part with his own. But when the globe came back he wanted to be sure he hadn't been cheated. An eccentric Englishman in a long coat had been called in. Both spheres, it seems, weighed practically the same. They both rolled the same. But somehow the stranger became convinced it was a fake. The boss then cut into it but it turned out to be solid gold.

Nevertheless, he *had* been cheated – a demonstration of which saved the Englishman's life. How had the Englishman done it? And what was the basis of the fraud?

10
Mixed Feelings

Anderson felt remorse for what had happened to Sherlock. But then he remembered how Sherlock had belittled him in front of others. Especially Sally. He had once said, 'Anderson here, on the basis that Hamburgers come from Hamburg, and that Beefburgers exist, would deduce there was a town in Germany called Beefburg.' That had really stung. And still did.

And then there was that time when, yet again, Lestrade had brought Sherlock to a crime scene.

'... and he's just lying next to a Paganini CD, the remains of a cold supper and half a bottle of red wine,' Lestrade was telling him.

'It's half a bottle of *claret*, actually,' Anderson pointed out. 'And what's *he* doing here? This is a crime scene. Put that down!'

Sherlock was holding the bottle up to the light, tipping it this way and that.

'You know you're not supposed to shake claret,' said Anderson. 'It unsettles it.'

Sherlock glanced at him. 'It's not.'

'Not what?'

'Not half a bottle. Just shy of half.'

'You're just guessing,' objected Anderson. 'And you're wrong. I believe in measuring things, not guesswork. I used a ruler.'

'And did you take account of the punt?'

'The punt?' gawped Anderson. 'We're miles from the river...'

How did Sherlock know that it was less than half a bottle, without using a ruler?

SOLUTIONS

I
Cryptic Clues

(a) Pathologists

(b) Sally Donovan

(c) Philip Anderson

2
An Obsession

The man had said 'jamás', which means 'never' in Spanish. As Sherlock has remarked, just because one interpretation fits doesn't mean it is the only one that fits. You only know you are finished when *all* the pieces fit. Which was appropriate, as Anderson was trying to fit all of the details of Sherlock's fall into some form which would allow him to have survived.

3

Missing Presumed Less Than 5 Foot 8

Sherlock had found there was an area of slight wear and tear where the suspect had stood when looking at himself in the mirror. Now a mirror needs to be at least half as long as the viewer is tall if he is to see his full height in it. It needs to be placed at the right height above the floor as well; it will also need to be slightly longer than half his height if he hopes to see the tips of his toes (which project forward), and by how much will depend on whether he has short feet or is wearing clown shoes. In conjunction, this all amounts to the deduction that the height of the suspect must have been less than double the length of the mirror. Sherlock measured the mirror and found it was 2 foot 10 inches long, doubled it and got an upper limit of 5 foot 8.

4

A Passing Observation

The lower shelf was spotless; the higher shelf had a little dust on it. Presumably the flat's occupant didn't see this from above and so was less prompted to dust it.

5

The Temple of Boom

(1 & 8), (2 & 7), (3 & 6), (4 & 5), (9 & 16), (10 & 15), (11 & 14) and (12 & 13).

6
Same Time, Same Place

Yes. Imagine Sherlock had a double able to duplicate his exact return journey but twelve hours earlier. Then, as the real Sherlock comes down and his double mounts, no matter what the details of their journeys, they are bound to pass each other. At that moment they are in the same place at the same time on the clock.

7
Two Temples of Tibet

The monk began with 63 amulets, and he left 32 of them each time he visited a temple.

Here's a rambling argument to lead to the answer. Suppose you have six pockets, and your donation of charms is d at each visit. Now run everything backwards in time. Instead of doubling between visits, you now halve; instead of donating, you now collect the same number of charms from each temple visit. You collect d from the sixth temple you visited and put it in your first pocket. On your way to the fifth visit, the content of the first pocket, d, is halved. You collect a further d and put it in your second pocket. You then lose half of what is in each pocket as you go to the fourth temple you visited. And so on.

It is clear that with six visits you need to halve what is in your first pocket five times. The total in your pockets at the end of this backward process is: $d + d/2 + d/4 + d/8 + d/16 + d/32$. (Note that the contents of each pocket are conveniently kept separate by the + signs; and the number of halvings the contents of any pocket is subject to depends on how many journeys between temples it undergoes in our backward journey.) Adding it all up we get $63d/32$. But this must be in reality C, the number of charms we started out with. The smallest d must be 32; the smallest C is therefore 63.

This walking-talking argument works, but if you prefer the algebraic approach here it is:

Suppose he starts with C charms and donates d at each temple visit. He arrives at the first temple, gives them d and has (C - d) left. On the way to the next temple, he doubles what he has and arrives at the second temple with 2(C - d). He then donates d, which leaves him with 2(C - d) - d. This is doubled on his way to the third temple, so he arrives there with: (2(2(C - d) - d), and he donates d, so he leaves with 2(2(C - d) - d) - d.

Continuing this process, we find after he has visited each temple three times he has 2(2(2(2(2(2(C - d) - d) - d) - d) - d) - d. This looks a little daunting. But you see the starting number C at the middle of all those nested brackets; you see the effect of the six doublings (in the form of the six 2s) and the six donations (the six minus ds). Well, if you multiply this out diligently, you find this equals $2^6C = d(2 + 4 + 8 + 16 + 32 + 64)$. Divide both sides by 2: $2^5C = d(1 + 2 + 4 + ... + 32)$; or: $32C = d(63)$. That is: $C = 63d/32$. Now C and d need to be whole numbers – it is in the nature of charms. If we want C to be as small as possible and non-fractional, we had better choose d to be equal to 32. Then C = 63.

8

A Crowning Achievement

The method rests essentially on a comparison of the density of the material from which the crown is made with the gold that made up the original.

The simplest way would be to measure the volume of the crown by submerging it and seeing how many ccs of water are displaced. Then weigh the crown and divide its mass by its volume. This gives you the density. If the density varies greatly from that of the gold the crown was made from, a substitution has taken place.

A more complicated way would be to weigh the crown in air and in water. Suspend it from the scale pan with a thread and let the crown submerge in a bucket of water standing on the floor, then see what weight now balances that. Archimedes tells us that a body in water (submerged or floating) is buoyed up by an up-thrust from the water equal in magnitude to the weight of the water displaced. That is why buoys will be buoys. In the case in point, you would weigh the crown in air, and then weigh the crown suspended in water (not sitting on the bottom of the bucket – why not?). With these two values for the weighing the density can be derived.

The density of gold is about 19.3 times that of water (about 1 gm/cc). If the traveller had not had this figure to hand, he could have requested a sample of gold and determined it by this method.

9

Yakuza Accuser

Sherlock had been snatched off the back streets of Harajuku and brought into the presence of the Yakuza boss – introduced as Yamamoto San (clearly not his name), short, suffering from halitosis and the owner of a cat – who insisted Sherlock check out the gold sphere, there and then, while the goldsmith responsible waited. Not having any lab equipment, Sherlock asked one of the men to strike the spheres with a mallet. Having a fine ear for music he was sure he could detect a difference in the sound. Sound travels differently in different materials. So without hesitation he pronounced the duplicate a fake.

But when one of the men cut into the sphere and the goldsmith trembled, it turned out to be gold all the way through. This enraged Yamamoto San, and he now turned his anger on Sherlock for damaging the sphere. Only the realisation that the first sphere must be the fake saved him. 'If you are wrong about this one, Englishman, you will die; first you damage my brother's present and now you risk mine.'

Luckily a bit of sawing and filing soon revealed a greyish core of what he assumed was tungsten. Tungsten is often used – plated with gold – to imitate gold bars. It is only marginally less dense than gold and is so much cheaper that it is often used in scams. Although he had solved the case, Yamamoto's mood had been so ruined by the damage done to both spheres that he had both Sherlock and the goldsmith dumped unceremoniously on the less salubrious side of Shinjuku.

10
Mixed Feelings

If the bottle were a cylinder with a flat base, it would be half-full if the claret came up to half its height, something which could certainly be determined with a ruler. But a bottle departs from this shape in two ways: the neck, and the punt (the name given to the indentation at the bottom of the bottle). When Sherlock took hold of the bottle, he marked the level of the claret with his thumb. He then inverted the bottle. If, after inversion, the level of the contents coincided with the level marked by his thumb, the volume of wine would have been the same as the volume of air in the bottle and the bottle would have been exactly half-full (and half-empty). If, after inversion, the claret came above his thumb, the bottle was more than half-full; if it was below, it was less than half-full. This procedure takes advantage of the fact that the state of being exactly half-full is a symmetrical state of affairs no matter what the shape of the bottle, in that if it's exactly half-full you can take the claret that was in one part of the bottle and replace it exactly with the air in the remaining part and vice versa. Of course, in what we refer to as a full bottle of wine there is in fact a small amount of air at the top. How does that affect matters?

THE
EMPTY
HEARSE

I
Cryptic Clues

(a) Where Sherlock caught a sort of rabies (6)

(b) You right rotters behave badly – sadists! (9)

(c) Technocrat provides Sherlock with this (6, 4)

(d) Where Sherlock hopes he and John could be honorably reteamed.
     (3, 10, 4)

2
Rebus

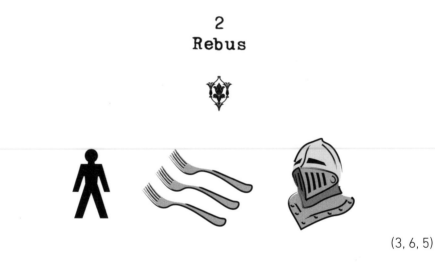

(3, 6, 5)

3
Rebus

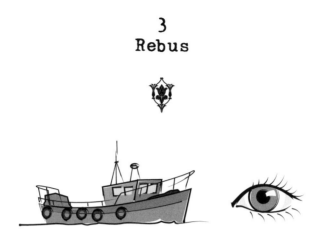

Part of Sherlock's improvised disguise (3, 3)

4
Cryptic Clue

Underground Network (3, 4)

5
Quiz

In the 'end' the one person that mattered the most? (5, 6)

6
Rebus

(7)

7
Dropouts

Each asterisk represents a missing letter. Find the word:

S*A*K*E*

8
The Shilcott Enquiry

'For example,' said Howard Shilcott, 'take the District Line train that came in before the anomalous one. Now 13 got off it at St James's Park and 7 got on, and I was able to calculate that there were consequentially 37 aboard as the train left St James's Park. It all adds up, you see. And that's as should be. So you can imagine how the last train has derailed me.'

How many left Westminster on the train Howard gives figures for?

9
Anagram

ARMADA TOURS – name of the mothballed station that Moran used in his attempt to undermine democracy (7, 4)

10
Rebus

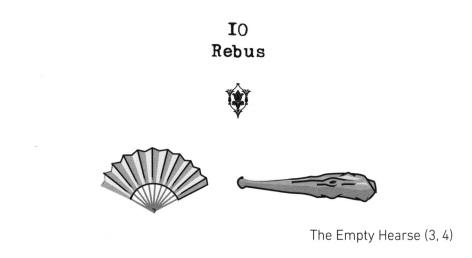

The Empty Hearse (3, 4)

II
Blast from the Past

There was a ping as a message arrived on Sherlock's phone. He frowned. 'I don't know whether this counts as a lie – or even whether it is true,' remarked Sherlock, showing John a picture from Moriarty.

John did a double take. 'But Moriarty's dead. What is this – a message from beyond the grave?'

'Well there are ways of arranging for message to be sent after your demise.'

'And there are ways of faking your own death,' said John flatly. 'But what does it mean?'

Well?

SOLUTIONS

I
Cryptic Clues

(a) Serbia

(b) Torturers (U + R + ROTTERS, jumbled up)

(c) Trench coat

(d) The Marylebone Road (at The Landmark, to be precise)

2
Rebus

Guy Fawkes Night

3
Rebus

Bow tie (boat, eye). He also added a little moustache and a pair of glasses.

4
Cryptic Clue

The Tube (Sherlock had initially assumed the 'underground network' referred to by Mycroft was a secret organisation.)

5
Quiz

Molly Hooper. She was rewarded with a kiss from Sherlock – and the offer of 'being' John Watson for the day.

6
Rebus

Bonfire (B on fire)

7
Dropouts

SPARKLER

8
The Shilcott Enquiry

43. This really is child's play and can be done in your head. The net change in the number of passengers at St James's Park was a decrease of 6; so there must have been 37 + 6 = 43 leaving Westminster.

9

Anagram

Sumatra Road. It was a coincidence that Sherlock referred to Moran as the Giant Rat of Sumatra.

10

Rebus

Fan Club

11

Blast from the Past

'Eye, shell, knot, die — "I shall not die",' pronounced Sherlock. 'Stretching it a bit, isn't it? Of course, if this really is from Moriarty, does it count as false because he is already dead? Or true, because he can't die in the future as he is already dead? It's a moot point. Or is it a way of saying that Moriarty is, in fact — and contrary to all appearances — still alive?'

THE
SIGN OF
THREE

I
The Riddle of Three

He was asked to be superlative.

He tried to be a little comparative, and he considered that his friend was comparative.

And finally Greg said he was a positive.

Who, how and why?

2
Cryptic Clues

(a) Was he a flat person? (3, 6, 6)

(b) An exceptional case, as Lestrade might express it; but particularly apt in this case (1, 6)

(c) Sort of rereading what Steve Bainbridge was (9)

(d) Walruses and weasels, apparently – or a hat! (8)

(e) The sign of 3? – sure! (8)

3
Same Difference

Identify the two words that differ only in the letters shown:

**** – What John hopes to do?

RA* – What the Poisoned Giant used?

4
A Real Corker

At John and Mary's wedding, Lestrade tried to cheer up a bored little girl with an old bar game. 'Now this one,' he chortled, 'is a real corker. What you have to do here,' he said, taking a wine cork, 'is drop this cork onto this hard surface so that it ends up upright.'

The girl at once took the cork and held it vertically less than a millimetre above the table and released it where it wobbled a little but remained resolutely upright.

'Ah. Right. OK. We better add a couple of ground rules,' laughed the Detective Inspector nervously. 'Let's say you have to drop it from higher than the length of the cork.'

And while she was dropping corks, he was able to wander off to the bar to refresh his own spirits and bring back his young charge a Coke. On his return, he was amazed to see she had mastered the knack. What was it?

Champagne Glasses

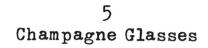

Next, Lestrade lined up seven champagne glasses in a row. 'At Hendon,' he explained to his audience of one, 'we used to fill them all, and if you wanted to invert a glass you had to drink the contents before you did – actually, you've already got a drink so I think it might be better if we forget that bit!'

'You did that on purpose,' she objected. 'And I *am* allowed champagne, just so you know. But you haven't told me what to do yet!'

'Oh yes,' continued Lestrade. 'Well, the task is this: we're going to flip these glasses so all seven end up face down. A move consists of flipping any pair of glasses you choose – by "flipping", I mean if a glass is face up it ends up face down; and if a glass is face down it ends up face up.'

'Flipping glasses. Is that what this game is called?' asked the girl. 'Doesn't sound that hard to me.'

'Well, here's the tricky bit. With each move you have to flip exactly *two* glasses – no more and no less.'

'Well, I'm pretty good at maths,' she told him, 'and I can tell you that's not going to happen.'

Why not?

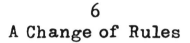

6
A Change of Rules

'Well-spotted!' cried Lestrade. 'As the hunter said when he caught sight of the leopard. Right then, young lady... Same set-up, but this time you must turn exactly three glasses per move. How many moves do you need?'

'We can flip six glasses with two goes,' she told him. 'But then we have an unflipped glass left over; so it must be at least three moves.'

Can you flip all seven glasses in just three moves?

7
An Extra Glass

'Now we've solved that,' said the girl, 'let's add another glass.'

'Eh?' Lestrade eyed one of the empty glasses and wondered if he could manage to refill it. Soon.

'We can flip seven glasses with three goes, and we can obviously flip nine glasses with three goes, as three goes into nine with nothing left over. So surely we should be able to manage eight with just three goes, too?'

Lestrade stared at her aghast. He recognised that sinking feeling he always got when he was in the same room as Sherlock: how had he got into this, how was he going to get out of it, and what was the answer to her question? They just didn't train you for this. 'You're a bit good at this, aren't you,' he told the beaming girl. 'So... Let's see...'

How many moves are necessary? And how are they to be performed?

8
Two Fractions

'How's your maths, Mr Lestrade?' the girl asked.

'Bit rusty. But I can generally get by with a bit of lubrication,' he said with a meaningful look at another empty glass.

'Well, this is a good one,' she continued. She jotted something on a napkin – two fractions:

$$999/1,000$$

and

$$1,000/1,001$$

'All *you* have to do, Mr Lestrade, is to say which is bigger.'

'Good grief,' replied Lestrade and began to do complicated things with common denominators.

His tormentor squirmed with glee. 'Do you give up yet?'

'No, I think I've managed to work it out.'

'Well, I did it in my head!' scoffed his rival. 'It's really simple if you think about it in the right way! Thanks for the Coke!' And she ran off.

Lestrade sat there scratching his head and looking at the result of the mess of calculations on the napkin.

What was the answer?

How had he arrived at it?

How had his rival done it?

9
Anagram

ACME VACATIONS – to Sherlock and John what 'Beth' is to Mary and John (7, 6)

SOLUTIONS

I
The Riddle of Three

It is Sherlock. He is the *Best* Man at John's wedding; he says Watson is the *better* man (because while Sherlock worked on the cases, it was John who saved lives); and, in *A Study in Pink*, Lestrade says he thinks that 'one day, if we're very, very lucky, he might even be a *good* one.' That hope Greg considers fulfilled later on in *The Final Problem. Good, better* and *best* are in grammar the positive, the comparative and the superlative forms of the adjective 'good'.

2
Cryptic Clues

(a) The Hollow Client (he was very flat indeed!)

(b) A belter

(c) Grenadier

(d) Bearskin (bear's kin, evolutionarily speaking)

(e) Positive (sure; the sign of the number 3, and the implication of Sherlock's 'Sign of Three')

3
Same Difference

CURE

CURARE

4
A Real Corker

If you try to drop it with the cork in a vertical orientation, the cork will bounce and topple onto its side. The trick is to drop it in a horizontal orientation. If you get the height just right, the cork will bounce up into a vertical position and stay there. It's a trick that needs a lot of practice.

5
Champagne Glasses

Let the state where there are seven glasses face up and none face down with the column:

$$7$$

$$0$$

We want to end up with seven glasses face down: that is in a state denoted by:

$$0$$

$$7$$

Any move makes two upright glasses face down; or two facing down face up; or takes a pair of glasses with one up and one down and simply changes the one that's up to down and the one that's down to up.

In the first case, we reduce the top number by 2 (and increase the bottom number by 2); in the second case we add 2 to the top number (and reduce the bottom number by 2). The last scenario leaves the number at the top (and the number on the bottom unchanged). That means the only tricks at our disposal are increasing or reducing the top number by 2 (with concomitant changes to the bottom number). But 7 is an odd number; adding or subtracting a 2 must always leave us with an odd number on top no matter how many times we do it (you can't make an odd number even by adding only even numbers to it!); so it can't be done.

7	5	3	1
0	2	4	6
0	2	4	6
7	5	3	1

Using our special notation, we have two sets of states. States *within* the same set can be reached by flipping pairs of glasses; but states in one set are inaccessible from states in the other set. The top row shows states accessible from the starting state 'all glasses facing up'; the lower row shows all the states accessible from the end position 'all glasses face down'. Mathematicians say the sets of states 'have different parity' so instead of calling this 'flipping glasses', we could call this Lestrade's 'parity piece'.

6
A Change of Rules

Adding and subtracting 3s is a different matter. Using the same notation as before:

$$7 - > 4 - > 3 - > 0$$

$$0 - > 3 - > 4 - > 7$$

The interesting step is the middle one. Note that you can only do it if you flip one of the glasses three times.

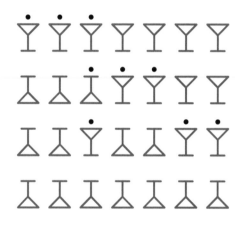

7
An Extra Glass

For eight glasses, our states are, in order:

$$8\ 5\ 4\ 3\ 0$$

$$0\ 3\ 4\ 5\ 8$$

And it cannot be done in fewer moves than four.

8

Two Fractions

1,000/1,001

Lestrade fell back on his dimly remembered maths lessons. He put them both over a common denominator getting the two fractions:

(999)(1001)/(1000)(1001)

and

(1000)(1000)/(1000)(1001)

He then remembered that a square is always larger than the product of the two numbers on either side of it and so deduced that 1,000/1,001 must be the larger fraction. [If the numbers are (n − 1), n and (n + 1), then (n − 1)(n + 1) = n^2 − 1, and this is less than n^2.]

The girl meanwhile, more creative and exploratory, thought in the following way: 999/1000 is 1/1000 short of 1; and 1,000/1,001 is 1/1,001 short of 1; so the second number is closer to 1 than the first and is therefore bigger.

9
Anagram

VATICAN CAMEOS

HIS
LAST
VOW

I
Riddle

What Molly gave to Sherlock's face for what she thought he had already taken? (5)

2
Same Difference

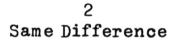

Identify the two words that differ only in the letters shown:

M*** (What Magnussen had)

P*** (With which he could operate)

3
Quiz

(a) In his day job, what would Dr Watson call Magnussen's sweaty condition? (13)

(b) What John used to save Bainbridge, and Magnussen used to manipulate his victims (8, 5)

4
(False) Memories of Redbeard

In his Mind Palace, Sherlock consoles himself by conjuring up images of Redbeard. The dog is running back and forth between the seven pillars of conventional wisdom and doing what dogs conventionally do to pillars – of wisdom or otherwise. The pillars are evenly spaced in a straight line. He starts from one of the pillars and runs directly to one he hasn't yet visited and carries on like this, back and forth, until every pillar has been visited once. If the separation between adjacent pillars is x, what is the greatest path he can cover?

5
Dropouts

Every second letter has dropped out of the word Sherlock used to describe what emotion is to him:

*B*O*R*N*

What is the word?

6
Rebus

What Sherlock did briefly in hospital (4-4)

7
Riddle

Why was Charles Augustus Magnussen like a flat battery?

8
Rebus

(9)

9
Enigma

What Moriarty said, but Sherlock could not have said to Mary!

SOLUTIONS

I
Riddle

Smack

2
Same Difference

imMunity

imPunity

3
Quiz

(a) Hyperhidrosis

(b) Pressure point

4
(False) Memories of Redbeard

23x. It might seem as if you should start at one end and go to the other end and keep zig-zagging to the most distant as-yet unvisited pillar. But that will amount (in units of x) to only $6 + 5 + 4 + 3 + 2 + 1 = 21$. Whereas if you start at pillar 4 and go to 7, from 7 to 1, from 1 to 6, from 6 to 2 , from 2 to 5 and 5 to 3, you have visited all 7 pillars and travelled: $3 + 6 + 5 + 4 + 3 + 2 = 23$ units. We'll leave you to figure out whether that is the best a dog can get and, if it is, why it is.

5
Dropouts

ABHORRENT

6
Rebus

Flat-line

7
Riddle

He had no vaults. (Volts? Get it? Oh, never mind!)

8
Rebus

Appledore (Apple, door)

9
Enigma

Did you miss me?

THE
ABOMINABLE
BRIDE

1
Enigma

Behead the singular and get a country.

Behead the plural and get a sign.

2
Cryptic Clues

(a) The street – or the magazine? (6)

(b) What muddled senile bluecoats demand at the Diogenes? (8, 7)

(c) Is he like Oscar – only more so? (6)

3
Plum Pudding, Plum Pudding

'I do so love plum puddings, little brother,' taunted Mycroft, when Holmes and Watson visited him at the Diogenes. 'Limited in form, I concede, but perfect in their own way. I do try to get Wilder to make them as spherical as possible and to stack them in triangular pyramids – just as I'm told they do with cannonballs, Dr Watson, though I rather expect shot and cannonballs are more your area of expertise than mine.

'Now, one plum pudding is a most uninteresting stack. But with two layers we get 3 + 1 = 4; and with three layers we get 6 + 3 + 1 = 10; well, you get the picture. Pile them high, say I. Yesterday he wheeled in two triangular pyramids one after the other and I said, "Wilder, you old fool, did you not realise that those two stacks could have been merged into one perfect triangular pyramidal stack? Why waste space and make two journeys?"'

How many puddings had Wilder brought Mycroft?

4
Sign Language

Watson's sign language was rusty, and he didn't like being mocked for it, so he fell back on the following:

As the doorman tried to detain him he touched the hair on his upper lip.

What did this mean?

5
The Sport

'And now,' continued Holmes, 'for difficulties in seeing what is there in plain sight. You will be in sore need of a diagram; and here is one I prepared earlier.' And he took out the picture shown.

```
WWWWWWWWWWWWWWWWWWWWWWWWWW
WWWWWWWWWWWWWWWWWWWWWWWWWW
WWWWWWWWWWWWWWWWWWWWWWWWWW
WWWWWWWWWWWWWWWWWWWWWWWWWW
WWWWWWWWWWWWWWWWWWWWWWWWWW
WWWWWWWWWWWWWWWWWWWWWWWWWW
WWWWWWWWWWWWWWWWWWWWWWWWWW
WWWWWWWWWWWWWWWWWWWWWWWWWW
WWWWWWWWWWWWWWWWWWWWWWWWWW
WWWWWWWWWWWWWWWWWWWWWWWWWW
WWWWWWWWWWWWWWWWWWWWWWWWWW
WWWWWWWWWWWWWWWWWWWWWWWWWW
WWWWWWWWWWWWWWWWWWWWWWWWWW
WWWWWWWWWWWWWWWWWWWWWWWWWW
WWWWWWWWWWWWWWWWWWWWWWWWWW
WWWWWWWWWWWWWWWWWWWWWWWWWW
WWWWWWWWWWWWWWWWWWWWWWWWWW
WWWWWWWWWWWWWWWWWWWWMWWW
WWWWWWWWWWWWWWWWWWWWWWWWWW
WWWWWWWWWWWWWWWWWWWWWWWWWW
WWWWWWWWWWWWWWWWWWWWWWWWWW
WWWWWWWWWWWWWWWWWWWWWWWWWW
```

'In this bank of Ws there is one rogue M; a snake in the grass, as it were. We say we see the picture, but the fact is we do not see everything; the brain fills in with what it assumes is there. The interloper can be found only by searching for it. It is a fair analogy of how I seek out the blip in the evidence on which the solution of the best cases so often depends.'

6
Top Hat

'So you see, Watson, seeing is a most unreliable sense. And that is the office that critical thinking and logic serve: as a corrective to our bad vision. So, if you know that what you think you see cannot exist, it is the side of logic that you must take and not that of mere impressions.'

'You said we are bad judges of what is there and what we see.'

'Ah yes,' mused Holmes. And he drew a picture of his top hat.

'So, Watson, you're a reliable witness. Is the brim of this hat wider than the hat is tall?'

Well?

7
The Maze

Holmes marched out of the house and straight into the hedge maze. Watson ran breathlessly after him.

'Now, Watson, the game is afoot. Tonight we will keep vigil and catch the would-be murderer red-handed.'

'Holmes,' protested Watson. 'We are in a maze.'

'It is always like that at this stage of a case. Oh, I see what you mean. I wonder if it has a centre or if it's just one of those where if you walk long enough you are bound to re-emerge where you entered.'

'I have heard,' ventured Watson, 'that if we place a hand to the right wall and follow that faithfully we must necessarily come out again.'

'You are a fount of knowledge, Watson, most of it incomplete knowledge. It depends on what kind of maze it is and what your goal. First of all, to make your rule of thumb work, you need to apply the principle from the very outset; and we are already some distance in. Second, if we apply the rule blindly and the maze is complicated enough we might go around in circles like lost souls trapped in Dante's Inferno. But since you imagine seeing is believing, let me draw a picture for you.'

He scribbled a simple sketch.

'So if we immediately apply your rule – left hand or right hand – to the wall, we will re-emerge, but we will have missed the goal: the dagger at the centre. If we fail to apply your rule from the outset and follow your rule blindly from some other point, we might be doomed to revisit the centre for ever and ever and never get out again.'

'But your maze is very simple to solve,' protested Watson.

'Oh, Watson.' Holmes spoke sharply. 'You have the advantage of the bird's eye view. It is not so easy from within. Secondly, if I can draw a simple maze that defeats your little right-hand rule, just think what a skilled designer of mazes can do!'

Draw a sketch of what Holmes showed Watson. Keep it simple.

8
A Hiding Place

Holmes and Watson tried several outbuildings and finally settled on the conservatory as it was at least warm and it afforded an excellent view of the bedroom windows of both Sir Eustace and Lady Carmichael. The two men fell into a sort of reverie as they waited among grafted apple trees in pots.

While Watson wondered whether Holmes was suppressing his attraction to women, Holmes focused on the shadow cast by a stack of four plant pots and whether that silhouette could be cut into two shapes that could be rearranged to make the silhouette of a plant pot twice the size of the four that make it up.

9
Cryptic Clues

(a) Shack suitable for gardener – or snooker? (7, 4)

(b) The pegs and props forming the apparition Holmes and Watson see (7, 5)

(c) What Ricoletti used to work the trick – and figure twice the size? (4, 6)

IO
The Moving Spot

In rehearsing their use of light and mirrors, the women's conspiracy shine a lantern slide of a tiny dagger onto a mirror and project the image onto the wall of Eustace Carmichael's home. The laws of optics demand that a beam aimed at an angle to the normal (the direction at right angles to the surface of the mirror) rebound at the same angle to the normal but on the other side of it. ('The angle of incidence equals the angle of reflection.') For the dagger to appear on Watson's face, the mirror has to be in the position shown. Through what angle will the team have to rotate the mirror to reflect the dagger onto Holmes?

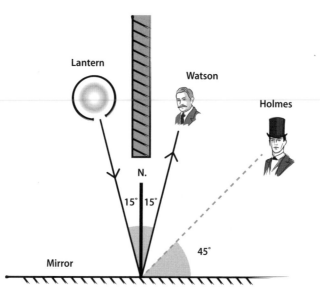

II
Inclined to Disagree

As the train sped on back towards London, Watson attempted to engage Holmes in conversation – if not about ghosts, then at least in some light-hearted banter. 'I have heard that one can deduce the exact speed of the train armed only with a watch and a knowledge of the separation of the telegraph poles,' he ventured.

'Really, Watson,' chided Holmes. 'First you insist on believing the evidence of your own eyes and not your brain, and now your ears are keen to believe whatever others tell you. There are conditions when knowing the exact number of telegraph poles you pass in a minute, and the exact separation between telegraph poles in yards will not give you a totally correct answer. Exceptional, of course, but it is the exception to a rule that so often proves the point about which a case revolves. And now, Watson, my good fellow, I need to commune with someone on my own level.'

'Who is that?'

'Me,' he replied.

So saying, Sherlock Holmes closed his eyes and assumed that peaceful state that Watson knew better than to break in on. And it irritated him, wondering what the conditions were that Holmes had referred to. Can you say?

I2
The Five Orange Pips

'Watson, do you still have Sir Eustace's orange pips about your person?'

'Indeed, Holmes.'

'Excellent. Kindly place all five in the three empty pillboxes you have in your bag so that each box contains a different odd number of pips.'

'With pleasure, Holmes. Hmm... That's another lot of nonsense, isn't it?'

'Not at all. It is simply an exercise in logic. And one that might take you long enough for me to have some peace and quiet on our journey back to Baker Street.'

13
The Appurtenances of Fame

The *Evening News* was running puzzles celebrating Holmes. Each row and column had to contain exactly one hat, one magnifying glass and one pipe. Any symbol at the end of any row (column) told you the first symbol you would see if you looked down that row (column) from the end at which the symbol appeared. Can you fill in the grid?

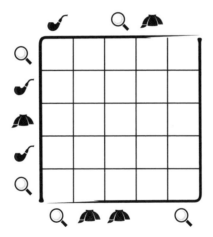

I4
Watson's Puzzle

Watson was pleased to note that the newspaper's second grid puzzle was even more complex: instead of symbols, each row or column had to have exactly one of the letters 'W', 'A', 'T', 'S', 'O' and 'N'.

'Clearly they understand the necessary function I fulfil in the solution of Holmes's cases.'

Can you fill in the grid?

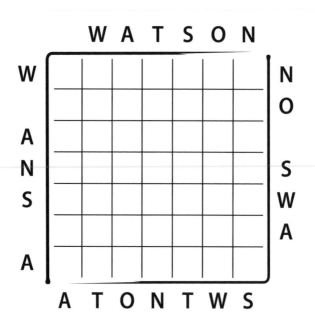

15
Rebus

Where Holmes retired to (4, 6)

16
Same Difference

The three words are identical in spelling except for the letters given:

******* (What John sometimes does for Sherlock and Mycroft)

****T*** (What Sherlock does as he 'awaits the devil')

****C*** (What John may do but Sherlock shouldn't do himself)

17
A Mysterious Message

'Somebody has a sprightly sense of humour,' remarked Holmes as Mrs Hudson brought up the mail. The envelope bore the name 'Reverend W. Wilks', and it contained fruit seeds of some sort.

'Good Lord, Holmes!' Watson cried in alarm. 'Now someone is threatening *you* with Death. But at least we have a name to go on. Wilks must be the intended recipient, or he is at the very least the one at whose hands your death is threatened.'

'I fear that line of approach will lead us in the wrong direction,' laughed Holmes as he placed it in his small collection of memorabilia.

Why?

SOLUTIONS

I
Enigma

Woman (Oman)

Women (Omen)

2
Cryptic Clues

(a) Strand

(b) Absolute silence

(c) Wilder

3
Plum Pudding, Plum Pudding

20. Numbers that can be stacked into a triangular pyramid of the kind Mycroft describes are called *tetrahedral numbers*. We have to hope the two pyramids were of the same size, as two pyramids containing 10 plum puddings (3 layers) give a pyramid containing 20 (4 layers), which

is within Mycroft's edacious capacities; whereas the smallest number resolvable into two different tetrahedral numbers is 680 (15 layers) = 560 (14 layers) + 120 (8 layers). [The first few tetrahedral numbers are 1, 4, 10, 20, 35, 56, 84, 120, 165, 220, 286, 364, 455, 560, 680, 816...]

4

Sign Language

Eye, 'ear, you = I hear you. And moustache = Must dash!

5

The Sport

WWWWWWWWWWWWWWWWWWWWWWWWWWWWW
WWWWWWWWWWWWWWWWWWWWWWWWWWWWW
WWWWWWWWWWWWWWWWWWWWWWWWWWWWW
WWWWWWWWWWWWWWWWWWWWWWWWWWWWW
WWWWWWWWWWWWWWWWWWWWWWWWWWWWW
WWWWWWWWWWWWWWWWWWWWWWWWWWWWW
WWWWWWWWWWWWWWWWWWWWWWWWWWWWW
WWWWWWWWWWWWWWWWWWWWWWWWWWWWW
WWWWWWWWWWWWWWWWWWWWWWWWWWWWW
WWWWWWWWWWWWWWWWWWWWWWWWWWWWW
WWWWWWWWWWWWWWWWWWWWWWWWWWWWW
WWWWWWWWWWWWWWWWWWWWWWWWWWWWW
WWWWWWWWWWWWWWWWWWWWWWWWWWWWW
WWWWWWWWWWWWWWWWWWWWWWWWWWWWW
WWWWWWWWWWWWWWWWWWWWWWWWWWWWW
WWWWWWWWWWWWWWWWWWWWWWWWWWWWW
WWWWWWWWWWWWWWWWWWWWWWWWWWWWW
WWWWWWWWWWWWWWWWWWWWWWWMWWWW
WWWWWWWWWWWWWWWWWWWWWWWWWWWW
WWWWWWWWWWWWWWWWWWWWWWWWWWWWW
WWWWWWWWWWWWWWWWWWWWWWWWWWWWW
WWWWWWWWWWWWWWWWWWWWWWWWWWWWW

204

6
Top Hat

The height and width at the brim are the same. The brain perceives vertical lines as longer than horizontal ones of an equal length.

7
The Maze

Holmes drew this trivial maze to prove that Watson's method might in general prove insufficient.

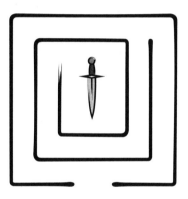

If you rely only on Watson's left-hand rule or right-hand rule, you will miss the goal entirely. If you only start to apply either rule by touching the inner wall that faces you as you enter, you will wander like a lost soul in and out of the chamber with the dagger in it without ever exiting the maze.

8
A Hiding Place

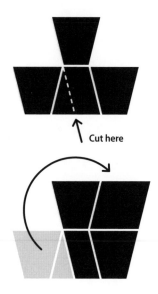

Cut here

9
Cryptic Clues

(a) Potting shed

(b) Pepper's Ghost

(c) Body double

IO
The Moving Spot

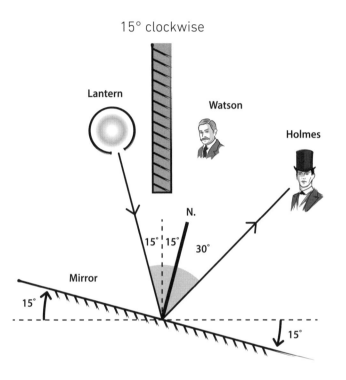

15° clockwise

Lantern

Watson

Holmes

N.

15° 15°   30°

Mirror

15°

15°

II
Inclined to Disagree

Holmes is being a bit picky here. If the railway line is on the flat, the speed (assumed constant) will be given by the number of posts passed in a unit of time multiplied by the distance between a pair of posts (assumed uniform). If the unit of time is a minute and the distance in yards, you will have the speed in yards per minute. Holmes is referring to the possibility that the train is on an incline. Then the horizontal distance between posts is not the same as the length of the line between them. However, since the greatest incline in the country is the Lickey Incline to the south of Birmingham where the gradient for about two miles is about 1 in 38 (2.65 per cent), the discrepancy in calculated speed will be at most of a similar order.

But then Holmes is inclined to be picky about assumptions. He himself prefers the clickety-clack method, where you count the number of clickety-clacks in a minute. Since he knows the length of rail, he at once knows the speed whether the train is on the flat or on a slope.

12
The Five Orange Pips

To avail ourselves of all the three odd numbers, 1, 3 and 5, we need one box to contain 1 pip, one to contain 3 and one to contain 5. But 1 + 3 + 5 is 9; so we need to count some of the pips more than once; the over-count we need is 4. How can we count some pips more than once? By nesting one box inside another. To get 1, we put a pip in one box; then to get 3, we just place that box inside one with 2 pips in it. To get 5, we just place the assembly of the first two boxes inside the third box which has the remaining two pips in it.

13
The Appurtenances of Fame

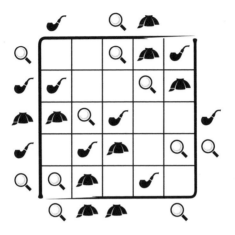

14
Watson's Puzzle

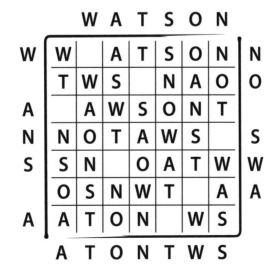

15
Rebus

Mind Palace [M in D; pal; ace]

16
Same Difference

MEDIATE

MEDI**T**ATE

MEDI**C**ATE

17
A Mysterious Message

As Holmes put it: 'Seeds don't have to be a symbol of death; they can symbolise renewal, interior development, growth. I suspect this is a token of acknowledgement from the, er, *Corps* of women. Well, Watson, they could hardly have sent me an apple: it would have been far too reminiscent of that other occasion where a chap accepted an Apple. And you know my aversion to the Fall.'

'But if it is from one of those women what does she mean by it?'

'Despite your greater familiarity with the fairer sex, Watson, I suspect you have less of an idea than I of what a woman means. That intelligence and sensitivity, which we far too uncomprehendingly and impatiently dismiss, is, I suspect, one of their principal attractions. But as for the name – and I warrant it is in Lady Carmichael's hand;

note the scent – you will find that Reverend W. Wilks is the name of a variety of *Malus domestica* – an apple. It is – to mimic her method of "say it with pips" – from a lady in her *Autumn Glory* whose *Maiden's Blush* I must spare.'

THE SIX
THATCHERS

1
Rebus

Quartet of mercenaries... (4)

2
Rebus

... and the country where they came unstuck (7)

3
Anagram

QUARANTINE HOODLUM – where Mary dies (3, 6, 8)

4
The Six Thatchers

Ajay believes his USB device is in one of the six busts of Mrs T. Before he starts on his iconoclastic project, what are the chances of it being in the last of the six that he examines? What are the chances of his finding it in the sixth after he has smashed the first five?

Now suppose instead that Ajay believes there is only a 60 per cent chance of the device being in the Thatcher busts at all. What are the chances it is in the first?

In the second, given it is not in the first?

In the third, given it is not in the first two?

In the fourth, given it is not in the first three?

In the fifth, given it is not in the first four?

In the sixth, given it is not in the first five?

Show that as he goes on – up to the last bust to be inspected – the probability the device is in the next bust, and the probability it is lost both increase.

5
Cryptic Clues

(a) Tong spared to reveal what Sherlock, Molly and Mrs Hudson are to Rosamund (10)

(b) Case of one trunk inside another? (3, 6, 5)

(c) Case of rare tyrannic hate? (3, 6, 7)

(d) The heart-stopping case – of a carter's cardi? (7, 6)

(e) Tricky memos about what Ajay seeks (6, 5)

6
Quiz

(a) What does Mycroft say has been slapped on the incident at Appledore? (1-6)

(b) What ice lolly does Norbury give as a possible favourite?

(c) What was odd about how John left the bus with the flower in his hair?

(d) What does 'Flekkete Bånd' mean?

(e) What are Kielbaski?

(f) How did Mary choose her destinations as she kept out of John and Sherlock's way?

(g) What narrative do Mary's attempts at avoidance echo?

(h) What game were Sherlock and Karim playing when Mary walked in?

7
Rebus

Members of Agra were this (9)

8
Bust a Bust

Sherlock decides to determine the lowest floor of a tower block from which a bust of Mrs T would break if dropped. He has been equipped with two identical such busts, which is just as well as, if he had only one, he would have to drop it from each floor starting at the first until the damn thing broke. He feels sure that having two identical simulacra of the Iron Lady (may she rust in peace) will make the task at least a little lighter. What should his strategy be to minimise the number of drops if the tower block has 36 floors? 22 floors?

9
Acrostic — John Reminisces

If you write the answers to the clues horizontally in the order given, the first and last letters each spell out the words clued in the Lights.

Clues (across)

(a) Lady Carmichael's first name (6)

(b) Sir —; is he head of Secret Intelligence Services? (5)

(c) — Sanderson Bank (4)

(d) Just the thing to hide in a forest! (4)

(e) Rest in peace for nasty chap from Kensington? (6)

(f) What Su Lin Yao worked in (11)

(g) Pair (3)

(h) It made even more of a mess of 221B (9)

Lights (down)

In *The Empty Hearse*, they discuss whether Sherlock is really dead.

SOLUTIONS

1
Rebus

AGRA

2
Rebus

Georgia (jaw, jar)

3
Anagram

The London Aquarium

4
The Six Thatchers

Before Ajay starts his bout of entering and breaking, the chances that the device is in any of the busts is 1/6. Once he has broken all the first five busts and not found it, the chances it is in the last are 1 (i.e. 100 per cent). The probabilities depend on the context.

First, note that Ajay's beliefs only affect the actual probabilities if he is right in his belief! Let us assume he is right. To deal with the case where there is a 40 per cent chance of the device not being in the six busts, we imagine four more busts that we cannot access to represent the concept of 'lost'. Now there are ten busts – six real ones and four imaginary ones. The chances of the device being found in any one of the first six (real) busts are 1/10 (i.e. 10 per cent); the chances of it being lost (i.e. in one of the four imaginary busts) is 1/10 + 1/10 + 1/10 + 1/10 = 4/10 = 40 per cent, as required.

If we don't find it in the first, the chances become 1/9 in each of the remaining five busts and 4/9 it is lost. If we don't find it in the second, the new probabilities per bust are then 1/8 (and chances 4/8 = 1/2 it is lost); with subsequent such disappointments we get chances:

1/7 for each of the three real busts; 4/7 it is lost;

1/6 for each of the two remaining real busts; 4/6 = 2/3 it is lost;

1/5 that it is in the last one; 4/5 = 80 per cent it is lost.

Finally, if it is not in the last real bust, the chances it is lost are 100 per cent.

Thus, as Ajay smashes bust after bust, the probability it is in the next bust increases (up to the last) and the chances it is lost also increase.

5

Cryptic Clues

(a) Godparents

(b) The Circus Torso

(c) The Canary Trainer

(d) Cardiac arrest

(e) Memory stick

6
Quiz

(a) D-Notice

(b) Mivvie

(c) He left by the front door

(d) 'Speckled band' (in Norwegian)

(e) Sausages (in Polish)

(f) By rolling a die

(g) *Appointment in Samarra*

(h) Happy Families, appropriately

7

Rebus

Assassins [ass, ass in S]

8

Bust a Bust

He should start by dropping a bust off the eighth floor. If it does not break, he should pick a floor seven higher, then the floor six higher above that and so on, finishing with the 8 + 7 + 6 + 5 + 4 + 3 + 2 + 1 = 36th floor. If the bust breaks when dropped from the eighth floor, he knows to check each floor from 1 up to 7 inclusive; that could take him at most eight drops. If it doesn't break from the eighth but breaks from the (8 + 7)th = 15th, he needs to check drops from each of the floors from 9 to 14 inclusive, which makes again for 2 + 6 = 8 drops. Well, you get the pattern. In this way, he needs to drop from at most eight floors to locate the floor from which the bust will break or if it doesn't break at all.

If there are 22 floors, Sherlock could locate the floor it breaks if dropped from (if it breaks at all) with seven drops.

Point to Ponder: If there is a flight of stairs going from each floor to the next, what is the greatest number of flights of stairs Sherlock is committing himself to climbing?

9
Acrostic

L o u i s **A**
E d w i **N**
S h a **D**
T r e **E**
R i p p e **R**
A n t i q u i t i e **S**
D u **O**
E x p l o s i o **N**

THE
LYING
DETECTIVE

I
Cryptic Clues

(a) Faith's father confessor? (9, 5)

(b) In what he hid? (5, 5)

(c) The sign of a weapon discharged? (7)

(d) Atropine spoiler sorted out by Sherlock (1, 6, 8)

2
Quiz

(a) It was playing when Mrs Hudson rolled up (3, 2, 3)

(b) Whence hailed the last of the Cryptic Clues? (4, 7)

3
Rebus

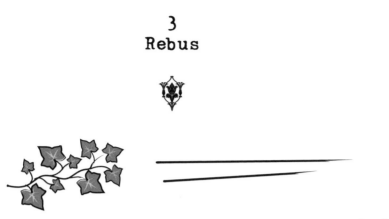

How the TD12 was delivered (2, 5)

4
Same Difference

Identify the two words which are spelt the same apart from the letters shown:

*O****** (malefactor)

*R****** (what he is now)

5
Russian Roulette

In his misery, Sherlock played Russian roulette in his Mind Palace (the only safe place to do it – do not try this at home). He loaded the six-gun with a single bullet and spun the chamber. What, he wondered, were the chances of surviving five 'clicks'? Then he would know the last pull of the trigger would be the last. When you have eliminated all the unlikeliness, whatever remains must be necessary. That about summarised probability, he thought.

And what if he spun the chamber before every attempt? What would be the chances of surviving five 'clicks' then? What would be the average length of a 'game'?

6
The Potters of Potters Bar

Culverton Smith has murdered before: a long time ago, he masqueraded with his wife as the Potters of Potters Bar. The Potters gave a party, and invited the Butchers, the Carpenters and the Shepherds. They all fitted nicely round the kitchen table. Mrs Potter let her husband arrange the seating. Apart from the usual constraints (no man sitting next either to another man or to his own wife), Mrs Potter helpfully reminded her husband that she didn't get on with the shepherd, and that Mr Butcher was not in the good books of the potter's wife. By the way, no one did what his name suggests. 'Easy,' said Mr Potter; 'I'll put Katherine Shepherd on my right.' What does the man sitting on the left of the shepherd's wife do for a living? Potter (or Culverton as we know him) killed the wife of the potter. What was her name?

[In this world, only men work, and all husbands get on well with their wives.]

7
John Says 'Goodbye'

As Sherlock lay unconscious there in Culverton Smith's hospital, John thought matters over. Giving him a good hiding in the morgue had released some of the pent-up grief he felt at losing Mary. She was gone; but she would always be with him. She was the true Treasure of Agra...

But Sherlock – difficult, infuriating, embarrassing, humiliating... He could almost hit him again, listing his shortcomings. But he was his mate. And Mary liked him. His single-minded focus on the thrills of the chase – like a drug – could be dangerous to those around him. He sometimes didn't seem to understand ordinary human beings at all.

If only that thing with 'the Woman' had come off. Instead of a r********* to this state, the master of d******** and the mistress of s*********! Oddly enough, all three words were spelled exactly the same way apart from the initial letters. Can you supply them?

8
Cutting Remarks

'All these cakes are £3.50 a slice,' said Sherlock. 'So why is that one £5?'

'Because that's madeira cake,' the woman behind the counter fired back.

Sherlock, John and Molly fell apart. It felt good to laugh after so much grief.

Molly pointed out the triangular cake. 'That's very "we three".'

'What if Gary turns up?' asked Sherlock.

'Greg.'

'Him too.'

'He'll just have to have the crumbs.'

'How are we going to cut it?'

'Three identical slices, Molly,' ordered Sherlock. 'One for each of our three musketeers.'

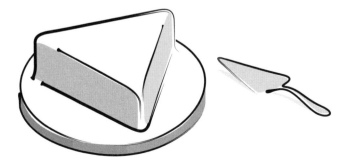

'There were four,' muttered John.

'Four what?'

'Musketeers.'

'Then why... Oh, not important. Molly! Three equal slices, please!'

Show how the cake can be cut into:

(a) three identical 3-sided pieces

(b) three identical 4-sided pieces

(c) four identical pieces

'Such a small cake!' remarked Sherlock. 'And yet it can still be cut into three identical pieces in an *infinite* number of ways.'

How do you know it can be cut into three identical pieces in an infinite number of ways?

9
By Text

Mycroft, squirming on Lady Smallwood's sofa, and drinking a glass of not very passable liqueur, excused himself to send Sherlock a text on John's phone:

81161625
29182084125
1292020125
21815208518
6181513 297
21815208518

'Why did he send it on *your* phone?' demanded Sherlock.

'Maybe he thought you'd erase it.'

Sherlock looked at the message and laughed. 'It seems our Mycroft is in danger of becoming human, too.'

What does it mean?

IO
Acrostic

If you write the answers to the clues horizontally in the order given, the first and last letters each spell out the words clued in the Lights.

Clues (across)

(a) The State of Liberty? (7)

(b) 'Nothing's "personal",' said this Colonel before a wedding (4)

(c) Culverton Smith exhibited this (4)

(d) The subject of this acrostic visits Sherlock in this (4)

(e) The equerry refers to the Queen as his — (8)

Lights (down)

Sherlock sized her up and got her number (5, 5)

II
Mrs Hudson Takes Control

(a) How did Mrs Hudson get the drop on Sherlock?

(b) Who's that on the wall?

(c) What does Mrs Hudson want Sherlock to get from the drawer?

(d) Where will she take him?

(e) In which car did she convey him?

SOLUTIONS

I
Cryptic Clues

(a) Culverton Smith

(b) Plain sight

(c) Gunshot (gun's hot)

(d) A triple poisoner

2
Quiz

(a) 'Ode to Joy'

(b) High Wycombe

3
Rebus

IV lines

4
Same Difference

POISONER

PRISONER

5
Russian Roulette

The chance of surviving five clicks assessed at the beginning are 1/6 as the bullet has to be in the only one of the six chambers that follows the one that the trigger is first pulled on. Another way to see this: the chance of surviving the first go is 5/6; of the second 4/5; of the third 3/4; of the fourth 2/3; of the fifth, 1/2; so that the chance of surviving as many as five clicks is the product of these: 5/6 x 4/5 x 3/4 x 2/3 x 1/2 = 1/6.

The chance of being taken out by each go is 1/6, assessed before we start, as there is nothing to choose between goes. The chances we will survive the next go assessed before each go, given that we have survived until then, are 5/6, 4/5, 3/4, 2/3, 1/2 and finally: 0.

The average length of a game will be (1/6)(1 + 2 + 3 + 4 + 5 + 6) = 3.5 goes.

If Sherlock spins before each attempt, his chances of losing are 1/6 with each go. The average number of goes we may expect to have before losing (including the fatal shot), n, will be given by: n = (1/6) x 1 + (5/6)(n + 1). This is because there is a 1 in 6 chance of the game ending after one go; 5/6 chance of surviving but then because we randomise the chambers again by spinning, we still expect on average a further n goes (plus the one we've already had). This gives an expected duration of the game of six goes. It follows, thought Sherlock, that it pays to spin if you want a long game.

Point to Ponder: If you put two bullets in adjacent chambers of your six-gun, would it still pay to spin before each go?

6

The Potters of Potters Bar

The man is a carpenter, and Potter (Culverton Smith), appropriately enough, is the butcher; he killed Katherine Shepherd.

Spouses must be three seats apart clockwise or anticlockwise. Listing participants from P to the right gives four possible plans without occupational constraint (with capital letters denoting the husbands and lower case letters denoting their wives):

PsBpCbSc

PsBcSpCb

PsCpBcSb

PsCbSpBc

Now for dislikes. Firstly, Potter is not a shepherd, nor are the men on either side of p. This rules out the first and third plans, as no one can be a shepherd. Butcher isn't a potter nor are the husbands of the women next to him, ruling out PsBcSpCb, as no one can be a potter. In PsCbSpBc, then, B, P and C aren't potters, so S must be. P and the men next to p (i.e. S and B) are not shepherds, so C is the shepherd. Now B isn't a potter, shepherd or a butcher: so he must be a carpenter, which makes P the butcher.

7
John Says 'Goodbye'

Reduction, deduction, seduction

8
Cutting Remarks

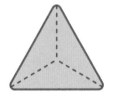

If you first identify the centre of the triangle and draw three radiating lines from it at 120° to each other (a bit like a Mercedes logo), you will automatically trisect the cake fairly: all three pieces will look the same and so will contain the same amount of cake. But this will also hold if you rotate this triad by any angle between 0° and 360° – an infinite number of angles to choose from. So the cake can be cut into three identical pieces in an *infinite* number of ways. Only when these lines fall symmetrically (go through the corners; or the midpoints of the sides), however, do we get nicely symmetrical pieces.

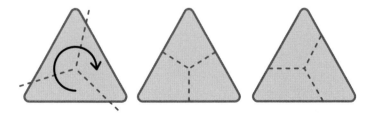

To cut the cake into four pieces, divide it as shown.

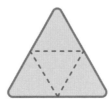

9
By Text

'Happy Birthday Little Brother – from Big Brother'. The letters have each been replaced by their ordinal number in the alphabet: so H = 8, A= 1, P = 16, and so on.

10
Acrostic

I n d i a n A

R e e D

E v i L

N u d E

E m p l o y e R

II
Mrs Hudson Takes Control

(a) She dropped the cup of tea Sherlock demanded she make. When she dropped this, Sherlock's reflexes made him catch it before it hit the floor. In the meantime she grabbed his gun.

(b) Culverton Smith. Sherlock was obsessing about taking this arrogant serial killer down, but he would need to get John's help first.

(c) A pair of handcuffs

(d) To John's new therapist's

(e) An Aston Martin V8 Vantage S – but she put him in the boot

THE
FINAL
PROBLEM

I
Age Old Questions

When Eurus was born Sherlock was 1 year old and Mycroft was 7 years older than Sherlock.

(a) When was Sherlock's age a whole number of times Eurus's age?

(b) When was the last time Mycroft's age was a whole number of times Eurus's age?

(c) When was the last time Mycroft's age was a whole number of times Sherlock's age?

(d) When did the total of the ages of Eurus and Sherlock first exceed Mycroft's age?

(All ages in whole numbers of years.)

2
Sherlock's Path

As a boy, Sherlock had carved his name into a wooden door. He liked to trace the letters of his name starting at the top and going down level by level with his index finger always proceeding to the nearest letter to the left or right of the one he was on. There seemed to be so many ways of doing it. How many ways are there of reading Sherlock in the array shown?

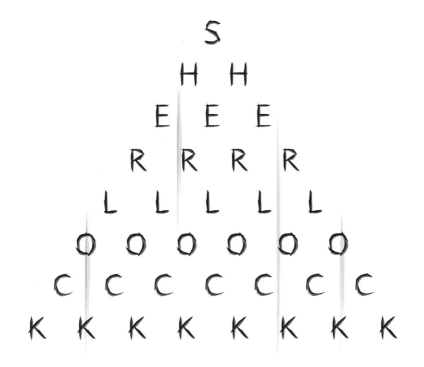

Mycroft's Way

Mycroft's effort at carving his name was more modest and symmetrical. How many ways are there of reading *his* name? In spelling you may only go from the letter you are on to the letter slightly to the left or the right in the next row down.

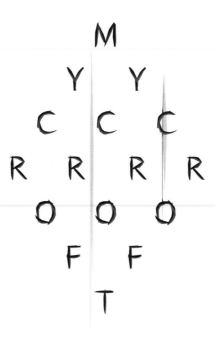

4
The Complexities of Eurus

The most complicated carving was inscribed by Eurus. In this you have to start at the top and can only proceed from the letter you are on to the letter immediately below it in the next row down or the letter to next on the left (if there is one) or the right (if there is one). How many ways of reading her name are there in the array of letters she carved in the old door?

```
E
U   U
R   R   R
U   U   U   U
S   S   S   S   S
H   H   H   H   H   H
O   O   O   O   O
L   L   L   L
M   M   M
E   E
S
```

5
Anagram

PERSISTENT CHARMS – for Eurus it was Moriarty's visit (9, 7)

6
Easy Come, Easy Go

Eurus is clever enough to leave Sherrinford whenever the fancy takes her. She has programmed the doors of the containment wing so that she can escape if she enters each room once. She starts in the room at the cell indicated in the diagram below. 'Inside, or outside. To me the words have practically lost their meanings,' she remarked.

Sketch a possible route.

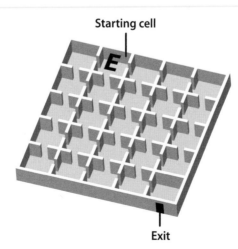

Starting cell

E

Exit

7
Cryptic Clues

(a) Doctor – and one that nearly did for Sherlock, John and Mycroft (5)

(b) How John's blog did – and what he – and Victor – did? (4, 4, 4)

(c) The way Eurus didn't get along with people and how Musgrave Hall sticks in the mind (4, 1, 5, 2, 4)

(d) The most serious ones were the clue to Eurus's singsong version of the Musgrove ritual (11)

(e) Study and note duet played (5)

8
Taking the Biscuit

As they picked up the pieces and gradually restored order to 221B, Mrs Hudson supplied them with tea and a packet of 26 ginger nuts. They played the old biscuit game: they each take it in turns to remove and eat one biscuit – or two. The one who takes the last biscuit gets to do the washing up. What is the strategy?

9
Anagram

BARONET CHAPEL – Where Sherlock and John finally exit, perfectly in step at last and on an equal footing. (8, 5)

SOLUTIONS

I
Age Old Questions

(a) Sherlock's age was only a whole number times Eurus's when she was 1 and he was 2. Their separation in age is too narrow to accommodate any further solutions.

(b) Mycroft, on the other hand, at 9 (Eurus, 1), at 10 (Eurus, 2), at 12 (Eurus, 4), and finally at 16 (Eurus, 8) was a whole number of times Eurus's age four times. Accordingly the last time was when he was 16.

(c) Mycroft was last a multiple of Sherlock's age when he was 14 (and Sherlock was 7).

(d) When Mycroft was 16, the combined ages of Eurus and Sherlock exceeded his age for the first time. Mycroft had always been the sensible older brother figure and it was important to Eurus when she and Sherlock would finally have him – as she thought of it – 'outnumbered'.

2
Sherlock's Path

128. Whatever letter you are on, there are two possible letters to end up on with your next move.

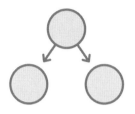

There are seven moves from the top to the bottom (not eight).
So starting at the top, there are 2 x 2 x 2 x 2 x 2 x 2 x 2 = 128 possible routes.

3
Mycroft's Way

20. We proceed in a slightly different way here. If there are x ways of arriving at a letter immediately above and to the left of a given letter, and y ways of arriving at the letter immediately above and to the right of the given letter, the total number of ways of arriving at the given letter are x + y.

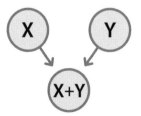

So we start at the top (you have to start there, so there's only way of getting there; so we write a 1 there) and write in each position the sum of the two positions adjacent to it in the line above.

The total number of ways of spelling out 'MYCROFT' is then seen to be 20.

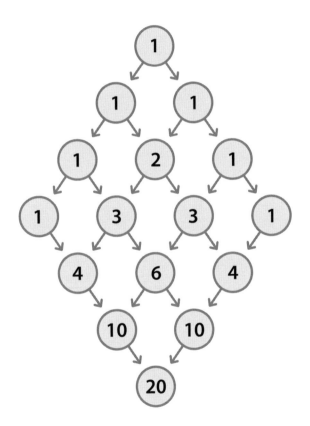

4

The Complexities of Eurus

2,188. This is just like the Mycroft array, only larger. The number in any position in this reformed array is obtained by summing the *three* numbers that are closest to it in the layer above.

1					
1	1				
2	2	1			
4	5	3	1		
9	12	9	4	1	
21	30	25	14	5	1
51	76	69	44	20	
127	196	189	133		
323	512	518			
835	1353				
2188					

5

Anagram

Christmas present

6

Easy Come, Easy Go

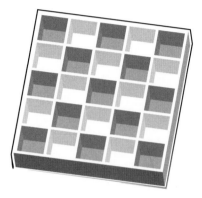

Eurus figures it out as follows. Imagine the cells have been coloured black (B) and white (W) like a chessboard, as shown. As you go from one cell to another, the colour will switch. So the colour of the cell you are in will alternate: BWBWB... if you start in a black cell; or WBWBWB... if you start in a white one. Now we see that the number of black cells is 13, and the number of white cells is 12. This extra B means our string of Bs and Ws which visits every cell just once has to start with a B, as it ends with a B. You may easily verify that, if Eurus starts from any black cell, it is possible to meet the conditions of the problem – with no problem at all. But Eurus starts in a white cell; and on the face of it this makes her task impossible.

But Eurus doesn't give up easily. The programming demands she *enter* each room exactly once and she must leave her starting cell to enter it. And you know how literal programs can be. This means if she leaves the starting cell and goes back into it, she has obeyed the conditions. That means she can count her starting cell twice: once as she starts from it; and once as she enters it. And that means in our string of alternating colours we have 13 Bs (for each black cell entered once) and 13 Ws (11 for each cell she enters once in the normal way; and two more representing the exceptional cell she starts from and then enters). That way, our string of colours will (a) alternate and (b) be 13 Ws long and 13 Bs long. And that makes the impossible possible.

7
Cryptic Clues

(a) Drone (Dr One – in the form of a quadcopter)

(b) Went down well

(c) Like a house on fire

(d) Gravestones (Gravest ones)

(e) Etude (E + DUET 'played')

8
Taking the Biscuit

Sherlock went first and took a single biscuit. That leaves 25 biscuits, which is (3 x 8) + 1. The point of this was that to win this game you need to present your opponent with a multiple of 3 (because 1 + 2 = 3) plus 1; then if he takes 1 you take 2 and vice versa, so that with each cycle of 2 goes where he has a go and you have a go the number of biscuits is reduced by 3. That means eventually your opponent will be left with one biscuit – and the washing up.

9
Anagram

Rathbone Place

Acknowledgements

For Mandy, who always finds the solution to every problem

Thanks, as ever, to Albert DePetrillo and Beth Wright at BBC Books for making it happen, and to Cavan Scott for helping to get it going.

ST

I am grateful to Zachar and Juju for their patience and for keeping me together in body and soul (what dishes!) while I was grappling with the infinitely layered masterpiece that is Sherlock; to Bob Cowley, whose Sherlockian skill is spotting the tiny detail others miss and yet never once straying into the inessential. To Steve Tribe for his deep knowledge and understanding of the Sherlockian myth; to Bethany Wright for turning the disordered scribbles and wild ramblings on the page into a book; and to Albert DePetrillo for his wisdom, creative appreciation and support.

CM